NIGHTMARES

THE SOJOURNS OF NIGHT

SHAHZADA ASFAQUE HUSSAIN ANSARI

Made with ♥ on the Notion Press Platform
www.notionpress.com

This book is dedicated to the loving memory of my late father...

Contents

Preface

I must begin by confessing that the poems in this collection may not cater to the tastes of the majority of the reading public, whose preference lies in poems about love, romance and nature. However, the fault is not theirs but mine. These poems, although conceived and inspired by various stages and events of my life, represent a realm far removed from the world of our daily realities. It is a realm where a forlorn soul struggles against metaphysical malevolence for its salvation, which remains as far-fetched and elusive at the end of the struggle as it is at the very beginning.

The present collection of poems, especially the four longer poems, although jovial by the very nature of their titles, represents the stark antithesis to that joviality within the domain of human consciousness. These poems explore the dark layers underneath the ever-shimmering surface of happiness and joy. They are basically poems of dejection, dissociation and disintegration of human sensibilities, which, although apparently modest, cannot forgo their primitive fears and apprehensions. They delve deep into the dark dungeons of the subconscious. Hence, they are as turbulent as the turbulence that characterizes that uncharted territory of human consciousness. The shorter poems, as all poetic creations are, reflective in nature, delineate the shades of anxiety, hypocrisy and deception onto the canvas of human emotions and experiences regarding love and romance. They exude a sense of utter resignation in the face of the impending catastrophe.

I sincerely expect the reader to find the experiences of these poems somewhat different, if not utterly unique. Through these poems, the readers will invariably strike a chord with the protagonist who becomes a symbol of the sacrificial lamb that all of us are forced to become at one stage of our lives or another.

Acknowledgements

These poems would never have been conceived until a few individuals in my life had succoured me into moulding my delirium and phobias into poetic creations. So, my deepest gratitude and indebtedness is due to my mother, Sabiha Khatoon and my mentor, Rabidev Mukherjee, without whose guidance I could never have been able to write a single syllable. Lastly, I am much grateful to my sisters and to that gentle breeze that blew by me whenever I sat in isolation by that blessed brook.

1. The Frost

My restless silence
Must find a voice
Serene and Sonorous
The unlettered and
The inarticulate
Now chase an expression
Unprecedentedly immaculate.

The signs of pain
And the symbols of joy
Pent up too tight
In a gaol where
No light could ever reach
Nor was there
Any air to breathe.

The destination of
My frozen expression
Appears too far
The passage is too long
And tiresome
Like the depth of darkness
Frightening and fearsome.

My alphabets are now
Lost or rest in peace
In an abyss deep
Bereft of any sound
And the mildest sheen
In sheer want
Of blood and veins.

The urge to be heard
Is now more pronounced
And the Truth
Now subtle and surcharged
Surges through the maze
Yet can't penetrate
The mighty misty phase.

So I wait for
The tender sunbeams
To fall and pierce
This glacial territory
And melt it to the core
And issue forth
The fountain of the Pure.

Thus will begin to flow
The brook thus frosted,
With Stasis's worms infested,
With the subtle shimmer
Of the sun rays
Imparting it beauty
And boon in many ways.

The world will, then,
Be wrought with revelations
Hitherto unknown
For the wine kept
The longer within the Earth's lap
The cozier it becomes
The keener with Nature's sap.

2. The Blessed Brook

Let this brook's water
Run pure and placed
Till the edge of Eternity
Without any break,
For it is indeed
A balm for Mankind
Wounded by its own axe
Sniveling, sobbing, shrieking
And no one's there to help.

We've ourselves amputated
Those generous hands
That once fed us
The tree of thorns
That we irrigated
With our kin's blood
Has now borne fruits
The cultivation of those seeds
Has earned largesse indeed
And here lies before us now
A lustrous harvest of thorns
A harvest of self-inflicting instruments
Ready to prick and pierce
None other but ourselves.

We bleed and bewail
With every prick,
Bathed in blood
We beg for succour
But in vain, alas,
Not a single soul to help
In this vast Wasteland.

But relief comes unexpected
From this blessed brook
That has been flowing unbridled
Inexhausted and inexhaustible
From the days of yore
Without any self indeed
For self destroys the self.

A steadfast companion
A perfect panacea
For all our bleeding wounds
An instrument for deliverance
Is this brook
Just a gaze at it
And it is there in you
And a calm, unprecedented
Seeps into the self
Through its ever-shimmering surface
Through its perpetually poised ripples
Of infinite proportion

Which lends a composure
Never to be found elsewhere.

So let this brook flow on
Purged and poised
For there will be many
Who will arrive
By chance perhaps
Bewailing and bleeding
With those very same
Self-inflicted wounds like mine
And receive a new lease of life
From its sacred water
Long after I'm but
A part of this benign Earth.

3. Ignorance

How I long for ignorance
The glorious blank
But not always hollow
The sign of having nothing
And the pattern of being nothing
A state of Being
Without the power of Being
An immersion into all
That comes unchecked
Unpaid and unsought
Like those thorns that,
Prior to the buds, sprout
And wraps the self
In a sable shroud.

How I long for that space
Though deserted by Grace
Where no sounds harsh
Reach the ears unhandicapped,
The state of lightlessness,
Dark but not dreadful,
Sombre but not suppressing,
Where no repugnant sight
Could ever penetrate the eyes

Through the mazy spines
To be etched onto the conscience
To be later derived
By the art of science
As the entity called Knowledge.

Sages of the days of yore
Were of a fabric all too pure
Weighing the sun and the moon
On the palms of either hands
Engulfing all of the Universe
Within their mind and heart
Knowing all that's there to know
And turning it onto Man
With a delicate tampering.

Now the sages ceased to be
From the mundane world free
And all that comes to us
Comes all too recklessly
All colours dark
All experiences, thorny and sharp,
That kill that
Upon which they feed.

So, to be left with nothing
Seems all the more endearing
But the dam is extinct
And the brook is all a-din.

4. Our Short Story

Sitting straight to me
She sometimes gives me a glance
She affects to remain calm
But I know it is not perchance

Sometimes, she evades my gaze
And tries to look composed
But she only deceives herself
For this composure is but forged.

We've been sitting there
For almost a year or so now
We've remained there static
Except for some courteous bow.

It was late Winter when I
Had the first glance at her
Looking over my shoulders
I looked perchance at her.

Settling my unsettled emotions
I hardly gave them a perusal
I thought it was a passing breeze
So, I wasn't stern in my refusal.

Thus, it all began and grew
Without ourselves being aware
Of what it may lead us to
It had such stealthy air.

Play and miss, play and miss
My eyes were equally restive
A whole season of joy went by
But my mood was barely festive.

Things calmed down a bit
By the time of late Summer
That sun reached its poignancy
My sun would scarcely glitter.

Our talks were a rarity
Often confused and indirect
For our emotions found vent
In no language, no dialect.

Confused and ever-confusing
Indirect but penetrating
Our conversations commenced
With a note too fascinating.

The language of our eyes
The syllables of our gesture
The rhythms of our movements
All had such furtive texture.

I burnt more from the heat
Within than from without
A pregnant cloud did appear
But relief I never sought.

Yet another turn of the season
The rain arrived with relief
It had some secret message
That reinforced my belief.

The soft breeze began to blow
The great invisible harbinger
That conveyed our souls
From the one to the other.

The quiet bank of that brook
Lent me a safe abode
From all the invisible injuries
On Love's prickly road.

The moon did get wet
Bathing into the brook's water
Still, her visage glowed
Upon that silvery salver.

Few tears we began to share
Yet still unknown to the other
Such pure and potent Elixir
As divine as heavenly nectar.

The day finally arrived
The day of celestial bliss
That reinforced our love-belief
And sealed it with a kiss.

5. The Disenchantment

I must rest in peace now
For the world is full of grief,
No consolation here whatsoever
Hence, life must be brief.

We are all but human
We do all but the good
We act rather too wisely
And in our foot wear our hood.

We are born, we are torn
From the womb too cruelly
Hence, we let out a cry of pain
But they take it as a cry of glee

There is colour, and the feast
There is beauty and zest
It's easy to delude yourself
And assume that you're blest.

Pale, plagued, perturbed,
I may now yield to anxiety
For nothing heals my wounds
And nothing brings me satiety.

Pestilence had eaten into
What we call the tree of life
Nothing now can resurrect it
Nothing can lend the lease of life.

There is agony and despair
There is anguish and anger
It's easy to presume that,
To them, we'll never surrender.

We are born, we are shorn,
On a head soft and bald
We take all the burden
Of this ever-hardening world.

We are all but ourselves
We have lost our conscience
We live like animals and
Boast of our grip of science.

Hence, life must be brief
For life is but a lease
And epitomizes anguish extreme
So I must rest in peace.

6. The Remains

I'm now but the remains
Of what I used to be
My self is caged in me
No one cares to set me free.

There was a time when I
Chased multi-hued butterflies
They held me captivated,
That fascination was my prize.

The sun glowed effervescently
There was hardly twilight
Darkness would never intervene
What was there was but light.

My dawns were imbued with
A potent and fertile exuberance
I believed I could overcome
All hostilities with perseverance.

I was ever-surrounded by
Colour, music, beauty and zest
Nothing looked ugly and profane
Everything was pure and chaste.

The vines of fruits, resplendent
With unborrowed colours,
Were so pleasing to the eye
So soothing were the birds' flutters.

The evening breeze caressed me
Ever so temperately,
I chased the dark nights
Vigorously, passionately.

The nightingale, from my side,
Unleashed notes of solace
She would cease at nothing
I bathed in the rain of Grace.

I bade the brooks to flow
According to my commands
They never disobeyed me
For Nature fulfilled my demands.

That jovial mood did
Never leave me unattended
I laughed the truest laugh
My zest was not pretended.

But something sore happened
I'm yet to know what
I'm no longer my older self
Something gave a cruel swat.

A drastic change has now
Come to define my condition
The sol of my exuberance
Now wears a dim complexion.

Subtlety has yielded to what
Has been the most unsubtle
When a flower is squeezed
We see the bleeding petal.

Of this abandoned orchard
I'm but a dying tree
No vine is laden with fruits
No bird now resides in me.

Dawn, morning, evening, night
All are now patterns of woe
I'm severed from my brook
I have lost my finest flow.

Dissociated, dejected, depressed
I stand by this still pond,
Watching the sun descending
Far into the horizontal blonde.

Battered from within and without
I'm now a coffin for myself
Laid inside this corporeal grave
I yearn for my bright self.

7. The Unrest

You sleep profoundly
I'm shrouded by numerous thoughts
Not always my own
Fighting, wrestling
Punching above my weight
To yoke them into subjugation.

The battle once started
Is never over
Never ever will it be
I'm fighting; you sleep still.
I yearn for you
Whenever the dark dawns
Or the daybreak disperses the dark
You remain indifferent as usual
Untouched by my painful longings
Still, I can't resist loving you
And you don't care still
Better be still in your slumber
Than to have a look
At my tempestuous self
Or spare a thought for it
Better be still, always still and supine.

8. Farewell

Farewell to my sweetest illusions,
My most serene vision
Of that world that never was
And never ever will be.
Yet it was, although flimsy
And invented out of fancy
Like some beatific phantasm
Begotten without resorting to sorcery,
But evolving out of
The tenderest of imagination
Through the mellow tampering
Of all that was
True, tender and temperate.

Now, let us part ways forever
Never ever to come across
Never to plague ourselves
Nor to please either
With a semblance of possessing
What we have been robbed off
Long ago in days past,
Whose phantoms, horrendous,
Still return to haunt my soul
Whenever there is, sometimes,

The pettiest possibility for me
To access tranquility.

My heart's blood keeps dripping
Upon this uncanny desert
Where roses bloom in a flash
Only to be metamorphosed
Into venomous thorns
At the most softest touch,
Where the hawk perches
Upon the prickly plants
And gnaws upon the carcasses
Ready to rot
Yet my blood never gives,
Irrigating the dead land still,
And ceases to be what it is.

So, farewell to the domain of dreams
The province of celestial beams
For now all that lies
Before my eyes
Is a burning waste
Erupted out of the volcano
Of that very rock
Which once lent refuge
To our tender passions
That roamed orphaned
Across the universe
Merely to find some peace,
Some fresh air to breathe.

9. Time

Time past and Time future
Both are seeds of anxiety
Time past is indeed the sum
Of all that made us
What we are or
What we are not or
What we could have become
If the past would have been
Like it was not.
Indeed, Time past conditions
Our Time present
And both become the womb
And the egg of Time future.

Time past is, at best,
But a catalyst into the present
The accumulation of all
That we have undergone or eschewed,
A puissant flood of yesteryears
Ever rejuvenated and revitalized
Primed to break into the fragile dam
Of the perennial present
Too powerful and pervasive
To be tamed by the ever-present now.

Time past is indeed never past
Nor does it let us go past
For rather like a spectre
It keeps chasing its undead target
And suddenly arrives and knocks
At the back of Time present.

Time future is indubitably
The most mysterious of the lot
Uncertain and undercover
And yet to be born permanently
Still pregnant sometimes
With those radiant hopes
And oracular optimism
That promise to never exhaust,
Or like a marvellous window
Opening onto some boundless territory
Of umpteen possibilities,
But sometimes, like an infant
Of the parents, past and present,
Begotten of a beleaguered birth
It unveils its blackened visage.

Time present is the only time
Concrete and palpable
Here and now only that we
Confront or are confronted
With the action of time
In the purest form
As to undo the past, sometimes,
Or to mould the future, at others,
Still unconditioned and unescorted
By the either.
It is at this moment
Of the never-exhaustible now
That we live and learn
And bear infinitely,
For this moment is never momentary
But eternal and immortal
The now is never dead
For it keeps resurrecting
From its own smouldering ashes
At the very moment it dies
Akin to the phoenix of
The mythological make-belief.

10. The Rest

Someday, I'll dig my grave
And lie down in it peacefully
May the Earth not accept me
But I'll fight with it gleefully.

There will be worms and insects
There will be scorpions and snakes
I'll happily surrender to them
For the Love of man is fake.

At times, on my bed at night,
In me ensues a loud uproar
Have I cheated on myself?
My heart begins to grow sore.

Love and lust lay on either side
And I'm sandwiched between them
Some say that both reside together
Some speak of the fight between them.

Joy leads to pain, pain to despair
Despair is not far from death
Do we die when we're actually dead?
What about life that chokes our breath?

I wait for the day at night
But that day is yet to dawn
Nights pass with my eyes open
And daybreak begets but a frown.

Some hazy forms do appear
But all too flimsy to perceive
I do run after them for
They might offer me some peace.

I'm a land with a quiver
And none chooses to reside on me
I can be restored to rest
If you put a gentle weight on me.

I'm not sterile, but fertile
Someone needs to dig into me
Once the upper crust is shed
You'll find a bliss in me.

But none ever dares to dig
Even though I offer them pearls
They think I'll deceive them
So they show me uncanny twirls.

'Listen, listen, listen', I cry
And none gives half an ear
None ever dares to approach
So gigantic is the power of fear.

So, let me depart with a handshake
I hope you'll not deny me this
This is all I can hope for now
Since you'll not allow me a kiss.

We come to this brown world
For everyone except ourselves
Here we perform fabulous tricks
To please everyone but ourselves.

I'll run faster than myself
For the clock keeps ticking
The slightest lack in pace
Will prove all too menacing.

There is no time to rest
This is no place to rest
It's incumbent upon us, dear,
To jostle to our final nest.

11. Sulphur

What chemistry lies unresolved
Between you and me still
That even a passing thought
Of yours begets
Pure sulphur in me
Which once was itself
A graceful sulphur
Gliding and glittering
Pleasing the mind and the soul
With its prismatic flight
That soared not far
Into the giant firmament
But skimmed gently
Within the periphery
Of the most verdurous
Orchard of my heart.

That orchard is no more
Its blessed abode
Since its enclosures
Were razed menacingly
By the mighty forces of the world
That chopped the gentle plants
Felled those mature trees
Killed the baby-birds
In their own nests
And sucked life out
Of every bough and leaf.

Once out of that orchard
It belonged to that
Ghastly world of zombies
A complete metamorphosis
Enveloped its being,
Those golden pinions
Appeared transformed
Into the scarlet pennons
Of that ghoulish army,
Those soft and tender eyes
Turned into the murderous glare
Of a hungry eagle
And that mellowed mouth
That once sucked nectar
Now sups at my heart's blood.

Thus that charming sulphur
Transubstantiated
Into pure sulphur in me
My heart is ablaze
My brain is aflame
My lungs are incinerated
My liver is calcined
And my blood surges boiling
Into every nook and corner
Of my furnaced self.

But once the fire recedes
A calm sublimated
Ensues at once from
The smouldering glow
For what was then gross
And terribly tainted
Within my unburnt self
Now seem sulphured,
Purged to the core
And that tiny sulphur
Resurrected and reborn
Begin to glide again
Within the circumference
Of my coveted soul.

12. Disintegration

The leaves are dried out
The boughs are dead
The flowers are withered
The petals have perished
The stem is still
The bark is diseased
The orchard is desolate
And the owl's hoot oozes
From the naked trees
The lake lay stagnant
Too filthy to reflect a shape.

This now bleak orchard
Was once an earthly Eden
With the trees overgrowing
Verdant and vibrant
With their fabulous foliage
With their sumptuous sheen
Sheltering those magnificent birds
Who, in their prismatic flights,
Or from their safe abode,
Outpoured their timeless paeans
In a voice so serene
That enamoured our souls.

We are now but the puppets,
Just the programmed selves
Controlled and commanded
By the animals within us
And doomed in a domain
Where the more is less
The greater shape it takes
And evaporates into Nothing,
Without even a sign of Nothing
Nothing proliferating further
Into a matrix of Nothing
And metamorphosed into
A simulacrum of Something
Something that beguiled us
With a simulation of Everything,
Everything that once was
The pattern of our Being.

Our perceptions are not sharp
Our determination is slippery
Ouractions are grisly
Our movements are stealthy
Our thoughts are filthy
Our skills are fragile
Our soul is sterile
The vein is frozen
That conveyed the blood
From our souls
To that of the Mankind

Into the soul of the universe.

Once severed from that Trinity
The self is robbed
Of that tranquility
That cherished us innately.
Instead, we now lie dormant
Within the corporeal graves
Of our very own bodies
Fed upon by the maggots
That once gnawed at others
Have now turned self-consuming
The carnivorous disintegrating
Further into the cannibalistic
Killing oneself to feed oneself.

13. Renunciation

I''ll not be a part
Of this foolish world
Where people bop to the tune
Of their animal passions
And call themselves gentlemen
I must part ways now
With this dreadful dazzle
That kills my eyes
And blinds me to visions of pure
And I see myself
As draped in costumes
Ideally filling to clowns.

I'll not be a part
Of this darkling world
Whose suns are all used up
The light that once
Illumined the darkest dungeons
Of our petty souls
Now but begets a silhouette
To obscure to be recalled
No faces but only masks
No bodies but only shadows
Borne not against light

But out of darkness absolute
Menacing us with
Their morbid and macabre shapes.

I'll not be a part
Of this sorry world
Where bats reign
And butterflies scream
A world of horrific dreams
Archetypally bereft
Of those celestial beams
That nurtured and nourished
The feeble and the meek
Transubstantiated into
An orchard verdant
With the devil's tongue
Where vipers and adders
Wait in hibernation
For their prey to step in.

I'll not be a part
Of this cruel world
Too brutal to withstand
With knives in every hand
With the smile of a child
Forged out of innocence, mild
The gyps of a fiend
Smoothened stealthily
Into the assurance of a friend

Augmenting the Time's trend
Of lending a creamy sheen
To the bread dipped in spleen.

Thus, I wish to escape
From this catastrophic world
Which has lent itself
To apocalypse imminent
Like an infernal volcano
Eager to find a vent
So I set sail
To the Elysium of solitaires
Who, disgusted with what
I've seen and endured,
Sought refuge in some shabby cottage
Far from the grisly territory
Of these emaciated zombies.

14. Fly and Taper

Little by little
Do I burn in you
My taper
Yet I have never complained
For you are the light
I must turn to
For my repose.

My life is but
An eagerness for death
I must hold you
In an eternal embrace
And shower countless kisses
On your countenance
It will ease my angst
Even if in this embrace
Is my death.

May you please to have
A quarter of mercy
Upon my anguished self
May you shy away
From burning me
But burn me anyway
For I'm destined to you
Whether you burn or spare
In your flames is my death
In this death is my rest.

Your gaze burns me
Your touch burns me
Your thought burns me
Your attainment burns me
Your love burns me
Your languishment burns me
Your movement burns me
Your stillness burns me
Your music burns me
Your melody burns me
Your rhythm burns me
Your pattern burns me

Yet, hardly ever I pour out
My sheer tender complaints
For I know, you also burn
Altogether, subjectively.
You don't burn me
Out of vengeance
But out of love
Tenderness saturated
Your flames are affectionate
Your burning me
Is but Love's largesse
An act of ultimate immersion
Into your own elements
Like an unconcocted potion
A union never to be severed.

15. Chaos

It's time for the prophets
To descend again
Not one by one
But together at a time
With all their miracles
Assigned to each specifically
To restore the world
For the world suffers a meta-chaos,
Cursed and condemned
Renounced and relinquished
Doomed and devastated
By those hands of Mankind
That once joined together
In supplication for salvation.

Those petty hands of ours
Are smirched with God's blood
Killed by our own sabers
Bleeding under our own gaze
Decomposing in the open
While the grave – diggers
Immersed in their task
Sing the eulogized requiem
But the very slight thought

Of its impending aftermath
The very premonition of it
Has frozen our marrows.

We, the assassins of God,
Have heralded a catastrophe –
The Earth is burning,
The firmament is ablaze
The oceans feed the fire
The air is aflame
The space explodes
With gigantic conflagration
The moon erupts at once
The stars shoot thunders
Of infernal proportion
And a metaphysical holocaust
Has encompassed the universe.

The revolutions of the Earth
Has begun to operate
Within our cerebral forts –
Eyes fight with hands
Hands wrestle with legs
Legs kick the brain out
The brain is at war with the heart
And the heart misinforms
Every artery and vein
And veins misguide the blood
Which surges within

Either all tor briskly
Or freezes rather too stealthily
And paralyses our tongue
Which fails to say 'Amen',
To our subterranean prayers.

The grand castle
Of this great civilization
Is crumbling apart
And all its enormous columns
Are deteriorating
Its base is trembling
Its buttressed walls
Are battered down
By the colossal fist
Of some cosmic malignity
Defiling all serenity
Defying all sanity
Deifying demi-godship.

So it's now high time
For the prophets to descend
All of them together
To bring God back
And reinstate him
On His celestial throne
So that the universe –
The minutest particle of it –
Is lit up again,

Is resurrected and restored
To its former benign state
And once again
We join our hands in supplication
And pronounce "Amen."
To the long-coveted prayer
That oozes out smoothly
From the heart of Everything.

16. Simulacrum

The presence is the absence
An absence in eternity
Enormous and eloquent
You are now but
A simulacrum of yours
A simulation of a simulation
Refined out of existence
To become too subtle and serene
Too delicate to be touched
Too tender to be loved.

You now belong elsewhere
Severed from my sorry self
Or surgeoned with
Such subtle scissors of time
As to show no sign
Of entwinement with me
A complete absence
Of me in thee
As if we never were
Together, whatsoever.

Time's untrimmed nails
Still scratch relentlessly
At my bare back
A whole fountain of blood
Erupts from my heart
With such might and force
With such untameable energy
That I'm awed and anxious
To be sapped.

Soon the time will arrive
And announce
A newly non-existent being
Of yours in me
As myself in thee
Then you'll perhaps
Taste the tincture
Of how it feels
To be renounced and relinquished
From all that once permeated
One's mind and soul
To be lost and forlorn
To be disjointed and dissected
From within and without
Nothing to anchor oneself
In this vast, trembling universe.

But for the time being
I feel connected still
For still could I find you
In the most deepest dungeon
Of my halloweened heart
From where sometimes,
Like an apparition, you rise
Without any recourse
To the paraphernalia of necromancy
But with the purest
And potent longings of my soul
Yet still a shadow
In the absolute absence
Of all that I can
Touch and tamper
Of all that can offer me
Solace and succour.

17. Our Love

Our old and aged love
Cannot brook hostilities
Anymore, forsooth,
But rather like a decrepit man
Of feeble limbs and muscles
Bent slightly from the waist
Coughing and wheezing
It approaches stumbling
The narrow grave.

Once it was adolescent and agile
Absolutely electric
And electrifying
And like a volcanic eruption
Of enormous conflagration
Fed by our own sulphur passion,
Unrestrained and awesome,
It made its way
Through the rocks and boulders
Of Time and space.

Still it was born gently,
Not a caesarean birth
By any stretch
But normal and natural,
Of the mutual embrace
Of our virgin hearts
That throbbed vehemently
Yearning to ravish
Or be ravished
To the fullest.

Further still, in its infancy,
It was cute and innocent
Rocking in the cradle
Of our tender emotions
Crying ever so sweetly
Beaming ever so softly
Unbaptized or uncircumcised
Still pure and divine,
An offshoot of some
Celestial form humanised
Teeming with energy
Potent enough
To subdue the universe.

18. Dasein

Every night at twelve,
It was a trend
With the tickling of the clock
He felt resurrected
Robust and rejuvenated
The barking of the street curs
Reinforced his vigour
He would brush and undress
Bathe in the boiling water's lake
And peel his entire skin out
And dispose of it in the lavatory
And put a new one on.

He would dress in a sable suite
Sprinkle the most pungent perfume
The polished shoes would glitter
Even in the abysmal dark
The scarlet necktie
Would remain suspended
Down to his naval
With elegance wrought with precision

And the wristwatch
Though long dormant
Would grace the hand
In proportion, transmundane.

The entirety of the universe
And the very nucleus of everything
Seemed to him his possession
Yet he dared not own them
The stars would extinguish
If he wished to touch,
The Earth would slide
Underneath his feet
Faster than his walking pace
And everything that was lit up
Would die at his merest gaze.

To wander onwards
Against the Night's Eternity
Was his sole errand
From the beginning of eternity
Which bisected between Night and Day
Would still be eternity
And the Night's Eternity
Is scarcely broader
Than the Day's Eternity
Neither the either Eternity

Lesser than the compound Eternity

And he was suspended
Between the two Eternities.

He would walk alone infinitely,
Against the rain and the gale
Against the mighty storms of hail,
On the paths forlorn
Of either hemisphere
On the days alternate
But he felt escorted
Followed and hounded
By shadows of all
Who he had dreamt of
During the full noon hour.

Consciousness or sleep
Or somnambulism deep
Or transcendence of mind
Or compulsion of Id
Or suspension of Ego
Or pretensions of superego
Or the mirror of the child
Or just crude fantasies wild
Led the holy sojourn on
Into the realm of the Unknown.

Now the seraphic view appears
Yet his approach was mingled with fears
The customary junction

Of this customary journey!
A beauty with a fright wrought
Slanted across the horizon
With elegance and precision
The first rays of dawn
Mildly beginning to be shown
Evolving from the dark
In contrast deep and stark
That offers solace to the heart.

A swarm of dragonflies
Of multiple shades
Began to skim gently
Over his sturdy shoulders
Circling over his high head
Reflecting the sunrays
Into prismatic proportion
All colours, bright and brilliant,
Resplendent with a metaphysical sheen
Encompassed his lonely figure,
And a surge of exuberance
Rushed through his veins
And he closed his eyes
To process the thrill within
And traversed every nook and corner
Of this vast universe.

Suddenly, a colossal serpent
Approached from the west far

And devoured the dawning sun
And, at once, all was dark,
And the dragonflies began
To scud back
To their safe abodes
But their meagre efforts
Were terribly terminated
By those multitudinous bats
Who shot off menacingly
From their headlong slumber
And instantly set off
Chasing those cute
And colourful creatures
And had their heads
Firmly placed in their mouths
And the rest of their bodies
Hanging loose and lifeless
As if suspended in perdition
For a span of time, timeless.

Now the predators of the dark
In the darkness of infernal chasm
Approached him quietly
And encircled him septuple
And, all at once, immobilized

Their relentless flight,
Stood suspended in the air
Before his stony eyes
With an uncanny simper
With their prey still in their jaws
And at their queer gaze
He evaporated out of existence.

19. Wilderness

I was once lonely and lost
In this wilderness
A man-forsaken domain
Where not a single human soul
To be seen ambling or trudging
In the pre-natal or posthumous state
Either cursed or canonized
Either fallen or flowered
Either damned or delivered
But my own solitary self
As renounced by humanity
As this wilderness itself.

But it wasn't that way always
I wasn't discarded always
I belonged, too,
To the human race
Which had cultivated
Compassion and conscience
Which had mastered
The art of science
Which never hesitated to call
A spade, a spade
Which was ever sustained

With the firmness of faith
In the Divinity's Grace,
Which always heeded
The values of transience
Which invariably accepted
The bounds of their lots
Which unscrupulously preferred
Being a generous host
Which never contemplated
Upon the idea of colonizing
Some great treasure island.

I was very much,
Quintessentially, a part of it
And it was equally a part of me
But then, all at once,
With an overpowering pace
Things began to change
That splendid fortress
Buttressed from each side
Garrisoning against
The army of ghouls
Began to crumble
And all of its inmates
Surrendered too meekly
And recoiled within themselves-
If they had any self left-

And refused to look beyond
Their own petty selves —
The petty became pervasive.

Since that Petty
Became all-encompassing
Since that Little
Became all-overpowering
Since that parasite's urge
To conquer the benefactor
Became Time's trend,
I was driven out
For they pronounced
That I didn't fit in
They deemed me out of shape
With what they deemed best
So I was driven out
Out of that world
Where the killing of Truth
Was all too common
Where Beauty was butchered
And Justice murdered
Where to be just
Was seriously censored
Where just to be
Was to be all but human.

So, I was banished from
What has now transformed
Into a wilderness itself-
A wilderness of lepers-
Diseased from within and without
Torn from the inside and the out
Uncared and ousted
By their own fellow species
And as lonely and lost
As was I once
In this vast wilderness.

Now I don't rue this exile
For that world no longer
Feeds my delicate yearnings
Instead I am endowed
With a blessed repose here
For here is no one to rejoice
At the pricks and the pain
For here is no one surely
To stab me in my back
For here is no one invariably
With daggers in smiles
Hardly anyone to deceive
The trust with guile
Exuding innocence infantile.

Of course, I barely lament
This sound aloofness
From that civilizational state,
For this abandoned territory
Adopted me unconditionally
And offered me its lap to rest.
Here in the midst of Nature
Overflowing with elixir
Pregnant with panacea
That cures the deepest cuts
And the most fatal wounds
And injuries inflicted by others
Or simply self-begotten
And caters to lend a poise
Never hitherto heard of
Or even ever conceived
Or slightly ever perceived.

Now standing here in the midst
Of this benign wilderness
Under the shade of this very tree
And its bought and its leaves
On this floor of raw soil
Which nurtures many a herb
And blooms many a flower,
I can lend myself to a prophecy
Of coming time, near than far,
Through a reflection of all
That went by me closely

That those who banished me
Will soon arrive here at pace
Being tortured and tormented
Being injured and inflicted
Being pursued and prosecuted
When they'll find in that world
No repose, no relief, no respite
Neither succour nor solace
And they'll see then
How eager is this wilderness,
To embrace their wretched souls,
Which they once denounced
As shallow and sinister
And how like a selfless mother
It accommodates them
And caresses them to peace
They might not have been able
To procure and purchase
With all their ways and wealth.

20. Happy New Year

They rang me up
And as I picked up the receiver
They said nothing at all
And kept me guessing
But I knew at once
Who they actually were
For I had no one left
To call me up
And the day being
The last of the year
Left not a jot of doubt,
For my phone rang
Only once in a year.

To lead me into disarray,
They instantly called out
Their names in succession
And burst into laughter,
A loud and lucid laughter,
But not an utterly
Unambiguous laughter,
Drastically disparate
From the innocent laughter
That we used to laugh
There in those meadows
In those lovely leas
In those open fields
On those high hills.

For the last many years
They called only once
On this very day
To wish me in advance
And it was not perchance
They had thus called,
For we, in our tender years,
Pledged to each other
To wish ahead of time
The arrival of the New Year
So far yet so near
Which every one of us,
Except me, held dear
For I had never seen
Witnessed or deemed
Any excess in my cheer
For I was no seer,
Perhaps, like my peers
Who always called me
And wished a "Happy New Year,"
Who always felt themselves
Unfettered, unshackled and freer.

But every year it thus went
When they had called
They never uttered a syllable
But when I spotted them
They only emitted laughter

NIGHTMARES

Never asked how I was
Or never told how they were.
In answer to all my queries,
In response to all my wishes,
What was all they could offer
Was an uncanny laughter.

But this was a year of change
They let out words in exchange
In a surcharged bassy voice
That actually sounded
Like a burst of noise
For they all spoke at once
Synchronising their utterances
Each with the other
Begetting a high-pitched,
Crude, cacophonous chorus.

At once, they all went silent
Over the phone call
Only an indistinct chatter
In a low, suppressed voice
Went on on the other side
Which I could distinctly hear
Yet could hardly comprehend
A single syllable of their mutter
Which again appeared
Nothing but restrained laughter
Out of which came

A voice crystal clear
Which was scarcely,
Indubitably, a human voice
Still could I make out
A once familiar tone
The rise and fall
The cadence and the tempo
The nadir and the crescendo
Of that sharp speech
Which did me beseech
To join them on
This great New Year's eve
In a newly opened mall
Whose name they didn't call
And kept me guessing
And pronounced prophetically
'To be there would be a blessing'.

Again, I ventured to ask
How would I identify
That particular mall,
For there had been inceptions
Of a few in recent times
But my close bosom friends
Were not be marginally moved
Hardly offered me a cue
And only belched out
A more explicit laughter
This time only slightly milder.

So long as I entreated
They only emitted laughter
Which, at last, incensed me
And I ceased to speak
And there was silence
Not a peace-begetting silence
But a deafening, dreary silence
Which sounded more starkly
Than our obscure utterance
Which subsumed itself into
The gigantic gloomy silence.

Thus silence predominated
For a span of time that seemed
Equal to a quarter of Eternity
After which a voice sharp and deep
Pierced through the void
And enlivened the talk again
And thus did dictate:
"Out of the town you move
Till the farthest North
Where all the roads end
And the forest extends
Its swiftly overgrowing size
Through the midst of which
Runs a dark, narrow alley
Which invariably takes you to
The epicentre of the woods
There you will get to see

The mall in all its majesty,
And there shall we meet
Dressed in attires neat
When the clock strikes twelve
We'll unrobe our quiet selves
But keep it a secret
From all the others
For even a mere mention
Sends down many a shivers
The mall is such a coveted place
None has ever reached it
Through the forest's mazy ways,
We will wait there for you
For a ball is long your due."

The call thus curtailed
Yet I blatantly failed
To grasp all the details
Of the protracted pronouncement
But only the mall remained
Within my cerebral domain,
And the time to meet
On New Year's Eve,
Only just nine hours left
To be there, to be blest.

A Herculean task it was
To finish off all my errands
All my good grand enterprises

To lighten all weight
Off my compressed self
To clear all my dues
To repent for all my sins
To relish all my victories
To concede to all my failures
To bid all my kin
Though they were long extinct,
A grand, solemn farewell
Forever, to be true.

Now was the time for me
To bid adieu quietly
And set off forthe mall
Leaving behind my kin all,
I came out of my abode
And turned around on the lawn
Had a full-frontal view
Darted queer questioning glances
And turned back all alright
My haven was scantily in plight,
I thought as I walked:
"Will it miss me tonight?
Or the days to come
Or the nights queuing to arrive?"
My mind was thus fraught
Between a 'yes' and a 'not'.
But the journey was long
So, such thoughts arrived

And long before gone.
Thus, the toing and the froing
The reaping and the sowing
The ebbing and the brewing
Thronged my solitary journey,
Spurred me on all a-going.

As I set out, it was twilight
But within a few moments
It was all night,
A dark, callous, coarse night,
An overpowering and gorging night
Yet I scarcely slackened my pace
And kept on prowling
Through the labyrinthine ways
Though not a soul could be seen
On the empty road
On the streets forlorn
On the deserted pavements
Over the long forsaken bridge,
Never a vehicle went past me
So I could entreat for lift
All the streetlights were off
So I feared walking wayward
And straying too far off
Into an uncharted domain
But I ploughed alright
On the scantily familiar road
And reached finally

NIGHTMARES

To the farthest North
Where all the ways converged
All, in one another, submerged
And from there emerged
The wilderness, in darkness, plunged.

Now, the journey through the woods,
In the night, on the foot,
Sent shivers down the spine,
Yet I had to undertake
Though with greater stake
The fearsome, fascinating trek.

As I entered the woods
It got enlivened with
A strange and mysterious life
The foliage expanded in size
The boughs unfurled their hands
The roots unchained underneath
The soft, supple surface
Which sent down tremors
Which disturbed greatly
My fast-moving gaits,
And then there ensued
The howling of the wolves
The yowling of the wild cats
The hooting of the owls
The croaking of the ravens
The growling of the jaguars

The braying of the jackals
The squeaking of the bats
And the last of them all
Was the hyena's laugh
All of these subsumed
Into a shrill, sinister sound
Encompassed me from all round
Engulfed me in trepidations
And suspended me in perdition.

So, I wished to hide
Behind a large, lustrous tree
Until all the voices subsided,
Unless all the sounds ceased,
But it was not to be
For all the nocturnal predators
Were stationed under a tree each
Slanting their grisly glances
Upon my slender physique
And as all were about to attack
There came a tiny pussy cat
Whom I had seen sporadically
On the lawn of my house
Waiting for its prey
In an eagerly still posture
And yelled a loud caterwaul
And everything was stalled-

NIGHTMARES

The movement and the sound
The tremors of the ground
The gazes of the hound.

The feline stood by my side
And looked up into my eyes
I reciprocated her glances
And then she started walking
Ahead of me as if leading
Through this milieu menacing,
And I ambled behind her,
Sloughing off all my fears,
Under the very predatory leers.

The cat led me on
To where my destination was
But never could I know
How she ever came to know
Where I was destined to go.

Eventually, we arrived
At the centre of the forest
Where there was an open space
Exuding a fine ambience
I felt as if entranced
And looked for the cat to thank
But she had disappeared
Vanished into the sylvan blank.

Thus, at last, I arrived,
Although late, around twelve,
And stood facing the majestic mall
All aloof from its surroundings
So detached from the wilderness
That it seemed to have pronounced
Sovereignty of its own territory
Within the periphery of which
Never a human soul
Could dare to come.

The mall was brilliantly lit up
With bright, effulgent lights
From each of its sides,
For it had myriads of gates
All opened far wide
All without a janitor
So eager to welcome
All its distinguished visitors,
Though from its outside front
It looked mildly sombre
But the light noise
Emanating from its interiors
Vouchsafed for the life
That went on inside.

Now, I approached the mall
Utterly drunk in gall
Tentative steps yet led me on

Quite uncertain of the door
Which was meant for me alone
Scampering from one to another
Like a rat in the sewer
Yet couldn't find the one bespoke.
Thus it went on and on
For a span of time, unknown
Until I reached a door
Where an old janitor sat
Who gestured to me
With his blurring blinking eyes
To enter from that scarlet gate
Which I did with haste.

Finally, I stepped into
That magnificent, majestic mall
Which from the inside
Looked more like the Harem
Of some great Ottoman Sultan
With the floor made of some
Exquisite ivory-like marble
And stepping onto it seemed
Nothing less than a sacrilege
And resplendent scarlet curtains,
Suspended at a uniform distance,
Reflecting a ruddy sheen
Into the exuberant ambience,
While the walls of the mall
Were all engraved with

Many a decorous shapes
Between which were etched
In bold, brilliant alphabets
The cabbalistic incantations
Along with various figures
Of occultist origins
One of them being
That of a tender lamb
Being prepared lavishly
For sacrifice to the gods or demi-gods
In order to propitiate their wrath.

Suddenly, I felt an intense urge
To have some water
For the hours-long walk
Seemed to have sapped me
Thus, I looked around
For the availability of water
But there was hardly any,
Yet I marked some stalls
Selling drinking water bottles
But such stalls were those
From which people queued up long.
Since my thirst was intense
So I jostled directly
To the lady on the counter
And entreated here earnestly
To give me a water bottle
Earlier than the others

For which I offered the price
Double or even quadruple
But she blankly refused
Scarcely gave a perusal
To my anxious utterances
And spoke thunderingly:
"Either you stay in the queue
Or I shall put the shutter down."

At this precarious pronouncement
All the people queuing up
Darted at me stern glances
So I, no longer capacitated
To countenance their glares,
Went to the tail of the queue
And, burying my gaze into the floor,
Stood there resignedly.

The queue moved slowly,
At an intolerably leisurely pace,
And by the time
I reached the coveted counter
A half of Eternity
Seemed to have passed
Whetting my thirst to extremes
And the very moment
I reached the counter
I cried out, "Water, Water!"
And handed the lady

A currency note of a hundred dollars
The lady looked askance at me
And emitted a simper
But instead of giving me
A bottle full of water
Offered me a wrapped parcel
Which I tore away instantly
And found a mask inside
Emblazoned with jewels
With diamonds and pearls.

I peered at the lady
Who scanned my agitation
With a crude, callous composure
And uttered nonchalantly
"This is all I have to offer."
And loudly called out, "Next."
Dismissing me with another simper.

I hurtled to another stall
And after which, another,
Immersed into polydipsia
Queuing up for water
Reaching the counter invariably
Only to discover that masks
Were all they had to offer.
But all the people around
Were content buying masks
Some of them even jostling

Hustling and bustling
Through the gathering
Sometimes overtaking
All the people queuing
To reach the mask stalls,
For it had dawned upon me
That there were mask stalls only.
They appeared in such a hurry
As if they would never find
Such serene serendipity
To buy those masks
Or the masks won't be
Available from tomorrow
If there was any tomorrow
To come tomorrow.

Barring their immaculate urge
To purchase masks in surge,
The propensity to achieve their goal
For which they took steps bold,
The contentment with getting the masks
A satiety deep and vast,
They scarcely looked happy
And exuded an impression
Of having been herded there
By some mysterious malign power
But what was most astounding
Was the sound of their voices
The phonetics of their speeches

Which coincided with
No language, no dialect
Known to homo sapiens
But with a queer laughter
Inherently crude, overtly softer,
That I was accustomed to
For many long years bygone
Although only over the phone
Or in the hours forlorn.

Now, the laughter recalled in me
The purpose of my journey
Of a robust reunion
With my close bosom friends,
Who was yet to be seen
Who in my consciousness
Were made of the elements of dream,
And just a flimsy prospect
Of its material manifestation
Had exhilarated me to extremes.

With calculated precaution,
Spurred with a keener vision,
I looked around and straight,
Sometimes over my shoulders,
Scanning each and every face
Which were all but all masked
With all-alike vizards
Jeopardizing my innocent lookout,

Yet I persisted and proceeded
With an ever sharper view
Still I could not figure out
A single soul I knew.

Suddenly, a harrowing bell
Boomed blaringly
And all the lights inside
Went off instantaneously
Everyone and everything
All encompassed in the dark
A blackness deep and stark
And a countdown commenced
In the reversal mode
In a hitherto unknown voice-
Still it wasn't a human voice-
Ten, Nine, Eight, Seven, Six,
Five, Four, Three, Two, One
And 'Zero' blasted us back
Into a domain of dim lights
Scantily enough to beget
Any silhouette of the crew
Barely enough to identify
A single soul I knew.

The New Year had arrived
And everyone in this crowd
Swirled into dancing frenziedly,
And I retired to an alcove

Witnessed the uncanny twirls
Of unidentified legs,
Some draped, some naked,
And then, one by one,
Each began to unmask
But their human visages
By now had metamorphosed
Into those of hyenas
Who leered hungrily at me
For I didn't fit in,
I shuddered at their glare
As they voiced out
A loud, raucous laughter
Which cut deep into the marrow
And I began to move
And they began to follow
All of them at once
I braced, they chased,
I kept running for hours
Yet I couldn't find
A solitary way out
Of this mysterious mall;
All its gates had disappeared
All the exits were blocked
Scarcely was there anyone
To lend me my friendly due
Hardly was there in existence
A single soul I knew.

Thus I went on ploughing
For a length of time
Surmounting to the whole of Eternity
A deep, dark eternity of anxiety
Until I arrived at the gate
Where that old janitor sat
This time only inside
Who, just sensing my approach,
Stretched his feeble eyes
Jerked his head in fright-
A not-so-unknown fright-
Although his very presence
Made my eyes beam bright
And lent a calm, although slight.

I hurtled to the old man
Besought him to open the gate
To avert an imminent fate
Implored him in a begging tone
In words comprised of
Honey, butter and foam.
First, he remained unperturbed
Or just affected to appear thus
But my persistent, poignant pleas
Eventually pierced his ears
And he raised his dropping head
And only darted jittery glances
And shook his head vehemently,
A gesture of refusing blankly,

But, then, I offered him all
I had hoarded throughout my life,
Still, he refused both,
The hoarding and pleas,
And shut off both his eyes
As if dying forcibly
But immediately after
He opened his eyes
As if surcharged with
A queer curious life
And looking into a blank
Voiced an injunction frank:
"It's perilous to cross the gate."
Yet, complying with my entreaty
He opened the gate scantily
And I thanked him heartily
And crawled through verily.

The gate did get shut again,
As I crossed it crawling,
Transporting me again
Into that dark domain
Of wilderness and bestiality
Yet I felt a repose
At not being munched and chewed
By those hyenas shrewd
But the repose was ephemeral
Like all the objects
Of this ever-decaying world

Imbued with life all too temporal
For I saw the forest
Had grown darker and denser
With all its denizens
Ever more ferocious and fearsome
And what contributed to the darkness
Was the wiping off the stars
And the extinguishment of the moon
Leaving the firmament
All too bare and barren
An unusually dismal terrain
Which ate into my composure
And I found myself closer
To a far greater danger.

My thirst reached its pinnacle,
A polydipsia that no other
Human beings have known,
And I went mad for water
Scampering again to and fro
Through the copse and the grove.

With failing eyes, I strove to see
Yet I couldn't spot
Even a jot of the life-source
And I hunched down
On the cool, grassy surface
And buried my head
In my fiercely quivering knees

And, at that very moment,
I heard a laughter-
A zestful, zealous laughter,
A familiar, friendly laughter-
I looked up and witnessed
Myself being encircled
By seven full-grown hyenas
Laughing at my face
And, through the language
Of laughter, seemed to say:
"We are your friends
Who called you invariably
On the day of year-end,
We are the ones with whom
You had spent the best days
Of your blithe childhood,
Though we are metamorphosed
Into what we now appear
Still, we hold you dear
You still are our best pal
So we invited you to the mall
Now we wish to incorporate you
Into our own element
To conscript you into
Our keen canine regiment."

I listened to the address,
Looking into the eyes,
Of my hyena friends

Who stared at my face
With a conspicuous gaze
But the one who spoke
Terrified me to the core
With his large, sharp cuspids,
But more than anything else
I was agonised with thirst,
A thirst which could make me
Guzzle a whole ocean,
So, I ventured to ask:
"May I have some water,
Else I may die in a fraction."
And the hyena spoke in reply:
"We can give you
Anything you wish for
But, first of all,
Conform to our proposition
Bow to us with veneration
And become one with us
Casting off your human lush."

Thus, I had to acquiesce
And ceded myself to them
At which all of them
All seven of them
Seemed saturated with elation
And emitted a loud laughter
In perfect synchronization
And asked me to follow them

And started ambling to the mall
Which we reached after
A long span of time
Like two Eternities entwined
And as the mall came into view
They asked me to lead the way,
Speak whatever I wished to say,
But I said nothing but "Water,"
To which they uttered "Better,"
And pushed me ahead of themselves
And warned me not to turn around
Neither to belch out another sound
But to keep marching on
Till the gate of the mall
Where a single solitary soul
Would offer me some water
The quicker I moved the better.

So, I proceeded at a pace
Without ever turning my face
But no sooner did I reach the gate
Than I felt that something sharp
Had pierced my calf
But I dared not turn back,
Within a fraction of a second
Something similar spiked
In the other calf
In both of my hamstrings
In the hips and the waist

In the back and the nape
Pulling me back forcibly
Munching at my flesh eagerly
Still I kept on plodding
Without, even once, looking
At the back or over the shoulders
For my eyes were riveted
To the gate of the mall
Where I deemed to find a soul
Who would lend me some water
But my pace slackened
Increasingly, at every step,
Until Icould move no more,
Dried with thirst, drenched in gore,
And crashed onto the floor
With a booming sound
And saw myself surrounded by hounds.

Thus, lying on the earth,
Peering at my hyena friends,
Who were still chewing my soft flesh
And still hungry for more,
I mustered my breath to speak:
"I did as you commanded
Offered you all you demanded
Conformed to all your proposition
Bowed down with utter veneration
Complied to become one with you
Is this treachery all my due?

I just asked only for some water
And is met with this gross banter
Have I hurt any of you?
Is this treason all my due?"

At this, the speaking hyena said:
"You conceded to be one with us
This is the process to be thus
Until from the human flesh freed
You can't incorporate into our breed
Not a treachery nor a treason
All is done with a sound reason
Unless you're entirely eaten by us
Never can you become one of us
This is a virtue, not a vice
It is indeed a blessing in disguise
Hold your tongue and let us eat
And be free from the human meat
Then be a part of our race
Be incarnated with a hyena face."

So they went munching on
All the flesh, all the bone
Until all my senses succumbed
And I ceased to feel
All the pricks and the pains
The blood coagulated in the veins
My eyesight became blurred
But the last thing I saw

Was the gate of the mall
Into which a window opened
And the old concierge peeped
And loudly called me names
"The bastard, the renegade"
And there was another roar of laughter
And the last that I heard
Was the sound of my own murmur:
"Water, Water, Water, Water......"

21. The Picnic

The picture in front
On the grey wall
With smiling yet stern faces
Looking at me all the time,
Following me, at times,
With strange queerness,
But, at others,
With utter nonchalance,
Frowning at me, at times,
Showering affection at others,
Never static as pictures are
But too buoyant with life
With an incomprehensible soul
Animated beyond exaggeration
And always escorting me
As if part of my entourage.

They invited me courteously
Into the verdurous orchard
Expanding in their backdrop
Asking me to hold their hand
And cross over into their realm
For a day's picnic.

The garden does entice me
With its infinite boundaries
The length of which seems
The journey of a day's sun
And the breath of which
Is equal to a full moon's voyage
Emanating an unearthly lush
And greenery of its own kind
Encompassing many a tree
In kinds various and sundry.

The copse of grapes and berries
Of apples and pomegranate
On the boughs of which
Sit and sing multicoloured birds,
Those little emissaries
Of the Nature's bounty
Whose eternal paeans
Do smoothen our souls
And solace our heavy hearts.

So they kept enjoining me
Until the day I yielded
And they were frantic with joy
Absolutely drunk in a frenzy,
They received me candidly
With a bow each after the other
Started walking abreast
Or escorting me diligently

Or carrying me in their laps
Or riding me on their atlas shoulders.

But so many strange faces
Engirdling me at once
Offering such favours
As appeared uncanny,
So I ventured to ask:
"Who are you all?"
And one of them
Came forward and said:
"I'm your father's grandfather."
Another one stepped ahead
And said unassumingly:
"I'm his father."
Another said:
"I'm his father."
Yet another one said:
"I'm his father."
So, the line of fatherhood
Extended reversely
Into the days of yore
Until a man appeared
Breaching through the crowd
Holding uprightly
A scarlet dagger
From which the drops
Of lukewarm blood
Were still dripping

And said thunderingly:
"I'm the father of them all.
I'm Cain, the scion of Adam."

He approached and offered
The dagger as a memento
Of this rendezvous
Which I mutely accepted
And there ensued
A shower of gifts
From each one of them;
Some gave me cakes,
Some chocolates,
Some offered ice-creams,
Some colourful teddy bears,
Some menagerie of metals
And some exotic articles
Made in antiquity
And yet to find a name.
Thus piled a large heap
Of the forefather's souvenirs
Which elated me to extremes.

Now was the time for a ride
The toy train lay stationed
On the farthest corner right
Of that grand orchard
Hitherto obscured,
Camouflaged with the foliage

Of the lustrous trees,
With neither the rail-track
Nor the mighty wheels,
But only two spacious bogies
Attached to the engine
With strings not clearly seen,
With no loco-pilot at all,
The train moved swiftly
In consonance with the command
Of the man who had proclaimed:
"I'm the father of them all."

Only within a few seconds
The train primed to its pace
With a passage so smooth
As to appear it barely moved
And, in no time, it seemed,
The orchard was a vision
Of some infinitely remote past,
And it ploughed into
A cavern deep and large
A terrain of abysmal dark
Which terrified me
And sent a shiver down the spine
Which went not unnoticed
By my guardian forefathers
And they began to sing
In a voice so shrill
That sounded like a sting;

The language of the song
Had never had I heard,
The cadences and the beat
The syllables and the feet
The tempo and the speed
All converged bleakly
In such perfect cacophony
That I felt under
The spell of dizziness
Though scarcely could anyone
Fathom my uneasiness
And went on singing
As if in a state of frenzy,
Immersed into euphoria
Of their self-begotten ecstasy
What transpired to them
Was that they sang a lullaby.

The train had its course
All the while
And now moved along
Into a chasm unforeseen
Like a snake crawling
Into dark, discarded bushes
Surreptitiously, stealthily,
And sounded so discreetly
Akin to the hissing
Of a snake under assault.

Here, even the foliage
Of the hitherto lustrous trees
Looked all the more menacing
Like a man dead by drowning
And discovered after weeks
And receiving its soul back
Again into that inflated skin
Terrifying even one's own kin.

The destination was, at last,
Within our vision's grasp
And the moment we arrived
Everyone was silenced;
Not a single syllable
Could be heard with precision
Only a low rustling sound
Perhaps begotten of
The rubbing of the leaves
And a spasmodic owl's hooting
Mingled with the sound
Of our heavy steps
Rising and falling in unison
As if in a rhythmic parade
And approached vigilantly
A splendid castle's gate.

Now came the twist of fate
A janitor of Hulk-like shape
Stood at the castle's gate

And greeted all of us,
Except only my own self,
With a courtly bow,
And all of my escorts
Now quickened their pace
Went past me in a flash
Each muttering something
In the other's ears
Patting my back
Uttering something to me
That I could barely comprehend
Yet I could construe
Their gestures and gesticulations
As a cold premonition
Of imminent tribulation.

So everyone went inside
The marvellous castle's gate
Leaving me behind
Out there in the pitch-dark
Of this vast wilderness
Although, once or twice,
They turned around
And looked at my plight
For I was just a sorry sight
Yet none of them
Adjured the commissionaire
To let me get inside.

However, it wasn't perchance
That I was thus abandoned,
It was in congruence
To that man's call
Who had proclaimed himself
To be "The father of them all."

So I was left forlorn
In front of that castle's gate
Peering at it with abject eyes
Pleading to be taken in
And then, with a
Tremendous thud,
The gate was closed
On my frightened face
By that inexorable concierge
Who did scarcely heed
My incessant, innocuous pleas
Scarcely ever looked
Towards my direction
Barely ever lent
The half of his ears
Although I offered him
All my gifts and souvenirs
And the very moment
That inimical thud arose
It served as a furtive code
To that castle's denizens
To extinguish all that was bright

So what till now was lit up
Was now bereft of light.

Thus woebegone sat I
Besides the large heap
Of the forefathers' largesse
And time began to fleet expeditiously
Some hundred years or so
The exact duration of which
I could barely know.
Was it for the real?
Or is it just the trick of time
That it plays in a man's mind?
Whatever it was
It was what it was,
And, as time passed,
The wilderness in front
Seemed denser than it was
And every now and then
Wild animals emerged
And came towards me
And started copulating,
In postures extremely riveting,
And then went away mutely
And got subsumed in the dark
Without launching an assault
Or even without
Threatening to do so,
Only taking with themselves

One of my gifts each
Until only the dagger remained
The unique memento of the man
Who had given the profound call
He was "The father of them all."

Thus time kept passing
But the night never did
For never did the sun rise
Nor did the dawn arrive
Neither did the stars appear
Nor did the moon once unveil
Its soothing silvery visage
And eventually after
Such exertions of the mind
It gave way, and I dozed off
Into such profound slumber
As was hitherto unknown
To the either of the two
Who resided in me,
And was instantly transported
Into a benign dream
Which was merely
A re-enactment of all
That had happened to me:
The picture, the picnic,
The forefathers, the souvenirs,
The Toy train and the journey
The orchard and the chasm

The castle and the concierge
The loneliness and the dark
The copulation of the beasts
The disbursal of my gifts.

But the dream went on
From the moment I dozed off
And saw a fairy bright,
In apparels resplendent white
With a magic wand
In her right hand
With two light wings
Suspended from her back,
Came close to me
And woke me up
With sweet-sounding swords
Whispered in my sleeping ears
And the moment I opened my eyes
The ambience was sunny and bright,
The fears had vanished
So did the panic-fright,
An unprecedented repose
A transcendental respite
Engulfed me to core
Offered me the soul's delight.

The translucent creature
Took me by my hands
Leading into the elusive castle

Which now appeared
As The Great Solomon's Temple,
The gigantic janitor,
This time, only bowed
As we stepped across
The magnificent castle's gate
And then we were greeted
By a large entourage
Of butlers and maids
Who took me on the excursion
Of this grand castle's interiors.

The castle consisted of
A hundred of rooms
Accommodated and enhanced with
Many an invaluable artefacts
But the most staggering
Were a series of exotic paintings,
Portraits of uncanny figures,
Marvellous, wondrous creatures,
With fascinating appearances
And intriguing postures
And at my inquisitive gaze
They all came to life
And bestowed upon me
Their benedictions bright
In such a rustling voice
In such an alien dialect
That I could scarcely comprehend

A single syllable
Of their obscure utterances.

Yet, puzzling in the equal proportion
Was the arrangement of light;
There were hardly any bulbs
With effulgence bright
Neither lamps nor tapers
Everything itself lit up
On whatever our gaze fell
Such was the disposition
Of all the hundred rooms
And all the while
During this excursion
The fabulous fairy
Held my hand tenaciously
And whenever I looked at her
She only beamed coyly.

Now she led me gently
Into the courtroom
With an enormous hall
With broad, majestic seats
Facing each other
On the either side
Through the midst of which
Went a wide passage
The crust of which
Was covered with

A scarlet carpet
Of celestial sheen
On which I was asked to step
And lead them on
To the magnificent throne
Forged of silver and gold
Bedecked with pearls and jewels
Embellished with diamonds bold.

She asked me to be seated
All the maids and butlers entreated
They draped me in a royal robe
And said I was their only hope
I was the one fit to be king
Began singing an ascension hymn
In long stretched syllables
To my keen ears palpable
Emitted sumptuous sonorous sound
And started moving in circles round
Now they held me by my hand
Every one of these cortege grand
Thus sat I on the splendid throne
Akin to Phoebus splendidly shone.

The subtle, solacing slumber
With the soothing, serene dream
The healer of my wounds
The panacea for my grief
Proved but all too brief

When the castle's gate
Opened with a severe thud
As jeopardizing as the one
With which it was shut,
And I was woken up
In the very midst of the night
With the sweet recollections
Of that fairy bright
And now was startled
With an uncanny sight
Imbued with nerves
Engulfed in fright,
For what my eyes saw
I couldn't believe my sight
For, as the gate opened,
Came a brilliant pool of light
I saw a boy stepping out
Robbed in attires lucent white
Followed by that very mob
Of the forefathers' sprites
Who had now put on
The attires of night
Led by that very man
Who had proclaimed with might,
Who had shouted that nefarious call,
That he, indeed, was
"The father of them all."

The crowd now proceeded
Towards my solitary self,
As they plodded closer
They gave a better exposure
To my beleaguered vision,
Now I saw the boy in white
Gentle cheeks and forehead bright
Rosy lips and quiet eyes
The silky hair gleaming
Though in the ide of the night
Was of my own visage and physique
And of my age and the sheen
Resembled me in every bit
When I sat on the royal seat
And stooped before me,
Looked at me with pleading eyes
Submerged in trepidation
Barely uttered a single sigh
Only entreated with meeker eyes
He wasn't even permitted to speak,
Such was the pinnacle
Of his plight's peak.

Now that hideous man appeared
Asked me where I had the dagger
Commanded me to take it out
And pierce into the boy's heart,
I looked up into his eyes,
Large, crimson, glowing, wide

Those seemed to have cast
A spell on my feeble mind
And I brought the dagger out
Smoothed it into the boy's heart
And he instantly faded away
But I felt pierced through
And a pool of blood ensued
From my own heart,
Yet I did not die
Only felt nauseated for a while
Then I got resurrected
Endowed with a queer life
A life that ripped me off
With all the senses of being alive
And with that man's gesture
All subsumed into oblivion
That I had hitherto known,
Seen, done or undergone,
And became a perennial part
Of our collective unconscious.

22. The Birthday Party

It was my first time
At her residence
And I was overwhelmed
Yet I felt such calm
As to be in transcendence
In a deluge of magnificence,
I put my best apparel on
The ones which were bespoke
For this long-coveted occasion
Like some dear possession.

I brushed my hair
Many a times too much
Gazed at my own image
In that magical mirror
Which never has yet
Reflected anything of shape
But only some obscure silhouettes,
My brand-new brown shoe
Just too good to my attire
Aligned with it commensurately
Lent me a look gentlemanly.

I walked through the streets
In the brilliant broad daylight
Through the glide of butterflies
Amidst the skim of dragonflies
Of various hues and textures,
The amble to her mansion
Seemed to be floating on their pennons
Imbued me with the feel
Of some majestic prince
Carving his way to Cinderella
Slaying the hideous demons
Beheading the mythical monsters
Bisecting the fabled ogres
Dissecting the grisly giants.

Thus I glided on and on
Beholding the beautiful views
Peering at the panoramic vistas
Of the world passing by
And after a long walk
Arguably the most serene
And tranquil walk
Of my hitherto tumultuous life
I felt somewhat fatigued
And steered off into an orchard
Which I found sumptuous
With copse of many a fruit trees
With groves of fascinating flowers
With a smooth passage

Leading through an arbour
To a placid and quiet pond
The water of which
It was resplendent with the shimmer
Of the fiery golden Phoebus.

I squatted down beside the pond,
Bracing myself against,
Under the very shade,
Of a huge banyan tree
And began throwing the pebbles
Sporadically into the pond,
Gazing at the ripples,
Which, starting at the centre ,
Expanded infinitely
Beyond all horizons
Of the pond-universe.
But within a few moments
There was a queer movement
Underthe surface of the water
Disrupting the ripple-patterns
As if something strange
Was sailing smoothly like a fish
Without divulging its countenance,
Its gills, the tail and the fins.

Stretching my eyes too wide
Didn't help me either,
I couldn't spot the creature

Failed to identify its stature
So I closed my eyes
And processed the repose
Into all the veins within
Which anaesthetized the mind
And I was transposed
Into a surreal sanctuary
And saw many a things
Hitherto unheard of
Or simply entirely inconceivable
Where memories, lived or suppressed,
Recollections, dear or detached,
Tuned themselves into images
Or into sundry patterns of images
Some obscure, some immaculate,
Flickering into ephemeral existence
And dying an immediate death
And then resurrecting again
Imparting joy and jitteriness
In quick sharp successions.

All these image patterns
Were ravished ravenously
By a frog's croaking
Trespassing into that territory
From a direction unknown,
I looked out all around
Scampered in all directions
For it appeared the croaking

Burst in from all sides.
To find the frog out
And put the croaking off forever
But the frog was nowhere
Within my meagre reach,
And the shrill clamour
Became increasingly intolerable
And I was thus startled up
Awakened out of my slumber
Thrust out of the trance
And spotted the frog there
Just by my left side
Croaking and smirking
Leering at my very face
And the moment I moved
My hitherto lethargic limbs
To brush the frog aside
It jumped into the pond
And promptly became one
With its pure placed water.

Now all was placid and serene
A tranquil materialization
Of a tranquil dream,
And, at once, the water swirled
Like a veiled hurricane unfurled
And three mermaids emerged
From the depths of the pond
And stood suspended

Half in water, half above
Darting innocuous glances
At my solitary self
And yet, uttering not a syllable
From their mellowed mouth
Still riveting my subdued gaze
To their own transcendent beauty
And time passed through silence-
Silence pressed into patterns
Of fascinating yet incomprehensible kind.

So, all of it thus went
In the quietude of Time's arrest
None of us spoke lest
One of the mermaids
Approached to ask in earnest:
"Who are you? What's your name?"
The second one followed suit
And enquired in a jolly mood:
"What's your errand? What's your game?"
The third one also did the same
With another query did me tame :
"Are you in love with a bright dame?"
To the first mermaid, I replied
"I'm a boy of mild disposition
My name is a matter of chance proposition."
To the second, I responded:
"My errand is just a long sojourn
My game is to pick flowers from thorns."

To the third, I retorted:
"There is nothing in it to hide
Yes. I love a damsel bright."

The moment I ceased to speak
They all began to giggle
And reciprocated words in whispers
And moulded the giggle into laughter
And then synchronised their voices
Into one clear accent and did utter:
"We are denizens of this pond
We three share a compact bond
Anyone who comes in its proximity
We hold him in dear affinity
We ask him the questions same
What's the name? What's the game?
Today, we added a question more
Just in case to be utterly sure
For your face and your look
Are strewn with words like a book
Your eyes tell many a tales
Of covetous courtship in verdurous vales
You are marching towards the flower
But beware of bats in the bower
Thrive to her with utter precaution
Or be ready for perdition
This is all we had to say
For all your stars are at bay."

Thus spoke the mermaid three
From the pond beside the tree
Moulding premonitions worst
In words bereft of curse
But it scarcely did me lead
Hardly I paid them any heed
And retorted in an assertive voice
To repudiate their murky bias:
"I don't heed what you just said
Although you tried all your best
To sow the seeds of unrest
Or to put me to some test
Releasing the vipers to the nest
Tormenting the host with the guest
I don't know at whose behest
You tried to pierce into my chest
And to extinguish all my zest
To injure my heart in my breast."

Here, the first mermaid cut me short
Spoke in a mild yet clear note:
"We didn't mean what you mistook
We're hiding nothing under the hood
We just said what we knew
To trust or not is all on you
We are not here to mislead
Just to beware you of your creed
We are not of the soothsayers
We belong to different spheres

You looked like an innocent child
Of looks pure and disposition mild
So we ventured to warn you, boy,
What you play with is not a toy."

This was all darted upon me
Here I quipped emphatically:
"She is not a toy to me
I'll not pay heed to thee
You don't know who she is
She is an emblem of a bliss
She is forged of elements pure
A panacea for the wounds sore
She is shaped in celestial mould
Eyes dark, skin silver, hair gold
She has such a purer mind
You won't find a parallel kind
Her heart is truth personified
A tongue that has never lied
From her eyes pours compassion
In overflowing, unfathomable proportion
Her hands are benevolence incarnate.
Her feet are made for generous gait
Her fragrance has a healing property
Can wean the lunatic from lunacy
Her comportments are solemnly wrought
Blissfully endowed, not foully bought
She has a voice soul-solacing
That can cure a mood menacing

She has a presence most assuring
She is made for lofty soaring
All the angels bow to her person
She is the nucleus of all attention
She is a goddess of magnanimity
She is a deity of cosmic pity."

My protracted proclamations
Did the mermaids' incense
Thus, the second mermaid
Did her speech commence:
"We are not with you at war
We just told what spoke your star
We don't possess an evil charm
We don't intend you any harm
We are not the witches wild
We are maids of nature mild
Did we call your beloved's names?
We don't play those naive games
We don't plant the rancour's seed
We don't have that devilish creed
You treated us with brazen defiance
So we won't invoke your compliance
That's your love and your life
What seems to be a sceptre is a knife
Deem of her as a damsel clean
Until you are swathed in spleen
Approach her with your blind eyes
Construe your deeds as action wise."

Here, the third mermaid began,
Her fiery assertions all at once:
"None has ever defied us thus
You do have an abnormal crush
You scarcely know what she is
Although you termed her as a bliss
We do know of her purer mind
Surely you won't find a parallel kind
We know of her truthful heart
Which is made of filthy dirt
The pitiful eyes and solacing voice!
That assuming gaze and raucous noise!
Her benevolent hands and generous gait!
Love them as much before youhate
We know what her elements are
She is made of poisonous tar
Her bearings have a solemn touch!
Never a soul pretended as much
She has an aroma so redeeming!
Don't worry, you'll soon be screaming
Her assuring presence and lofty soaring!
She has a soul soul-devouring
Not the angels but Satan's crew
Do bow to her, it is true.
Neither a deity nor a goddess
She is indeed Lucifer's mistress."

"Enough is enough! Shut your lips
Or I'll punch you for your glibs
Are you mermaids or the Devil's disciples?
Don't you have the slightest of scruples?
You burst my heart with your words
Now I'm sure that you are cursed
What pents the creature to a pond
That belongs to the oceans blonde?
It's your trade, it's your craft
To beguile the blokes with your shaft
You can't stand the smell of romance
Hence, you begin your infernal dance
Deemed of you utterly otherwise
You have cut my heart to slice
Tarry I'll not a moment longer
You have such an insatiable hunger
You feed on our gentle affections
And play games with tender emotions
Many like me may have been nabbed
But I'm not the one to be trapped
I'll not take the rancour's cup
Your efforts have only braced me up
I will love her all the more
She is indeed a damsel pure."

Thus, I got up perspiring
And started ploughing
Towards the exit of the orchard
To abandon the place in a hurry

And, then, from my back,
The first mermaid said:
"You may put your sword in sheath
Guard your heart from her teeth."
The second mermaid picked up:
"Fight with us, with anger seethe
Guard your heart from her teeth."
The third mermaid followed suit:
"Go and love her as you breathe
Guard your heart from her teeth."

These premonitions I heeded not
And scampered briskly
Back to the barren road
But the walk seemed uphill,
For the passage had overgrown
With sharp, thorny thickets
So, I decelerated my pace
And trod with utter precaution
In a very alarming fashion
Watching over my footfalls
As not to step over
On the tail of some viper
Who might be taking a nap
In the dark, dense bushes
Or just simply sloughing off.

It was almost twilight
When I stepped out
Of that occult orchard
And shot a dolorous glance
At the old aged sun,
Kissing the western horizon
With its sombre rays
Which lent me composure –
A composure with which
I, in the morning, set out
On this auspicious sojourn –
And I smoothed my attire
Which has been creased
And tied my shoelaces again,
And with a tranquil heart
Brimming with ethereal hopes
Wrought with celestial trance
Set off I with gentle pride
Through the mazes of romance.

Thus, another long march ensued
During which the full moon
Rose in all its grandeur
Accompanied and escorted
By the multitude of stars
On the sable canvas
Of the gigantic firmament
Under which I ambled
My way to her mansion

Reflecting upon the memories
Of our first meeting
Of the first chance touch
Of her smooth ivory hands
Of the first piercing gaze
Of our hitherto evasive eyes
Of the tempestuous placidity
Of our virgin hearts,
Of the succinct proximity
Of our quivering bodies,
Of the queer incapability
Of uttering a single syllable,
Of the harsh deception of time
Of the stern obstinacy
Of not parting too soon,
Of the avalanche of rebellion
Of our brewing minds,
Of the first mutual tears
Of our eventual parting.

Yet all these tender whiles,
Something gnawed at my heart
And the poise did me evade
And there, instantly, I knelt
And, to the Almighty,
I made long prostration
Spelt words of supplication
And besought to grant me
The tranquillity of bygone memories

Of those tender recollections
On which my naive heart
Had so succulently feasted.
Then I was up and walking
Under this overarching past
Murmuring and babbling
Incomplete phrases and words
As if in an act of rehearsal
In order to ward off scruples
In the moment of materialisation
Of this long-coveted union.

At last, there it was
Her great grand mansion
With seven enormous columns
Over which on the frieze
Were sculpted out
Shapes of carnivorous beasts
But with the faces of man
On the top of which
Rested a large pediment
Of splendid ivory texture
In the lap of which
Was etched out in bold letters
'INAMORATO'S ELYSIUM'
Which in the moonlight
Was exquisitely visible
Although artificial lights
Of multiple colours

Lent their sparkling services
At regular yet stark intervals
Dying the emboldened letters
Orange, brown, emerald
Blue, violet and crimson
In commensuration to the hue
That flickered and died
And was succeeded by the other.

The large palatial door
Stood in my full-frontal view
And stole an accosting glance
At my innocuous presence,
So I pressed the bell button
And the whole mansion inside
From the roof to the floor
Reverberated infinitely
Till a fairy-like figure
Clad in resplendent white
Opened the door ajar
And surveyed my countenance
Which made her shrunken eyes
Expand ritualistically
Into one bright, beaming mould
And she pulled the door wide open,
Enjoined me to step in
Through the language of her eyes
Through the words of her breathing
Through her pure heart's beating

With such perfect precision
In such fine crescendo
With such subtle syllables
In such rhymes and rhythms
In such feet and meter
With such music and melody
As to seem a sonorous poem.

She grasped me by hand
And stood close to me
In sheer precise proximity
That constituted a memory of past,
So close that I felt
The warmth of her respiration
Her mild hibiscus aroma
The fragrance of her hair
That invigorated the deepest recess
Of my hungry soul.
Her visage seemed,
Though slightly transformed
From those long bygone days,
Still well beyond all affinities,
Diana or Venus
Helen or Hera
Aphrodite or Athena
Penelope or Phoebe
Might still, at best, partake
In her grand majestic entourage.

She led me through the stairs
Down to the underground floor
Through a narrow passage
Into a very dim stretch
At the end of which
Was a door which opened
Into a spacious bedroom,
With illuminating gadgets
Lending it a brilliance
In absolute stark contrast
To the passage we just paved,
In the very middle of which
Was a large round bed,
With a tester of polypropylene mesh,
Suspended over its circular shape
From the infinite ceiling,
Towards which she beckoned me
And enjoined me to rest
After the day's long journey
Which initially I gainsaid,
And there she grasped my hand
And took me to the bed
And squatted down on it
And, lying me down, held
My long-burdened head

In her maternal lap
And started voicing out
That very melancholic lullaby
With which, in my childhood,
My mother lulled me to sleep.

Thus transposed was I
Into a blank sleepscape
And dreamt of nothing
No faces or images
Appeared in that terrain
Nor was there anyone
To push me off that cliff,
Hardly any of the beasts
That hitherto conjured up
Chasing me in cold blood,
Barely was there that shadow
That invariably escorted me
Through those gothic castles,
Scarcely the infernal brook
Swarmed with legions of serpents
Which I felt forced to cross,
Scantily the pinnacle of thirst
In the vast sunburnt desert
In the midst of which
My solitary figure meekly stood,
Rarely the poise of slumber
Marred and molested
By grotesque, gruesome voices

Of the hell-bound necromancers
Perennially invoking Beelzebub,
But only soothing sleep,
Sleep coupled with peace
And tripled with tranquillity
And quadrupled with serenity.

The long-coveted slumber
Lasted for a centennial
Or a little more than that
Or at least it appeared so
Until an umami taste
Tampered with mild sweetness
Penetrated my open mouth
And roused me up
And to my utmost nonplus
I found myself enamoured
In a fervent liplock
Which I wished to prolong
With my conscious consummation
But the moment she felt
The duress of my lips
She flinched away instantly
And coloured conspicuously
But I grasped her hand
And showered kisses
On the back of her palm
Which she tried to forgo
But merely sheerly assumingly.

She tripped down rhythmically
From the regal bed
And started dancing'
With commensurate movements
Of her hands and her legs
Of her neck and her waist
Of her eyes and her breast
To which my gaze
Was so tenacious riveted.
It was, by no means,
A weird, frenzied dance,
Not of the licentious kind,
Neither the ballet nor belly dance,
But only mild movement
Of all her parts in unison,
And I approached her
And grabbed her from behind
And began sideways movements
In perfect synchronisation
With her own nimble legs
And here she started to sing
In measures profuse
A song from a legendary romance
Which I had never read
But only faintly heard of
From some sources unknown.

Now I had the leisure

To inhale the fragrance
Of her jet-black hair
Of her pristine body
To my heart's content
Which penetrated profusely
The deepest recess of my inside
And lured me into
Vigorous acts of lovemaking
And I kissed her ears,
Her temples and all around
But the moment I licked
At her pure satin nape
She pirouetted and hugged me
And heaved involuntarily
A series of turbulent sighs
Which made me encompass
The succinct rise and fall
Of her maternal bosoms
Against my disquiet chest
Against which my heart
Pummelled and kicked
Or banged its squidgy head
In uttermost vehemence
Which, all the more, spurred me
To compress her further
Against my own frissoning body
And the moment froze-
All sounds were silenced
All movements were stalled-

Into one perfect epiphany
Of our unconcocted union
Of the poise of synthesis,
Of our hitherto divergent selves,
Of the zenith of saturation
Of our unravished emotions,
Of the metaphysical power
Of our subtle togetherness,
Of the attainment of Nirvana
Through the attainment of the other.

I unzipped her gown
From the backside
Which made her cleavage
Conspicuously discernible
To my devouring gaze
And I smelled her bosoms
Each after the other
And rested my head
In the middle of them
And the clock struck twelve-
Twelve long, sibilant ringing
Ensued at uniform intervals-
And I, without raising my head,
Whispered my birthday wishes
And was about to unleash
The hungry dogs within me,
The door of the room opened
And three crossbreeds stepped in

In decisive parade-like gaits-
The first of them was
Half goat, half hyena
The second of them was
Half gazelle, half jackal
And the last of them being
Half sheep, half wolf-
And silently stationed by
And glowered at us
Which sent many a shivers
Down my meek marrows
And I embraced her tightly
At which she only chuckled
And patted me to composure,
And at the conclusion of which,
The triumvirate, concurrently,
Belched a prolonged yell
And, thereupon, my beloved-she
Curtailed her embrace
And turned towards them
And followed them straight
Out of that queer room.

The moment she stepped out
Slamming the door closed
On my very own visage
A loud cacophonous roar
Arose and encompassed
Every nook and corner

Of that splendid mansion
And raucous music pierced
Into my very own ears
Striking a deafening cord
Which hurled me to compress
My ears with my hardened hands
Though the screeching noise
Did not last too long
Yet the buzz remained
Reverberated and echoed,
So I approached the door
And peeped through the keyhole
And spotted a rabble
Of vicenarians and tricenarians
In the act of frenzied dance
With music, colour and wine
As if in a moment of delirium
Throwing themselves around
One upon another
And, once in a while,
Smashing onto the floor
Through the excessive twisting
Of their inebriated legs
But the dim sparkling lights
Dissuaded my meeker gaze
From cognizing their countenances
And the electrifying ambience
Absolutely switched me off
And I was left forlorn

And barely in the mood to feast,
Although it was unapologetically,
The very first party
Or any of the like celebration
That I had been a part of
Or had just remotely witnessed
For a decade or so.

Thus, it went on and on
For many an hours long
Unmarred and uninterrupted
Deep into the night
But towards the proximity
Of the apprehensible dawn
Just before the rooster's call
Or the owl's return to its abode
Or the bat's diurnal slumber
All the noises and voices
Subsumed into silence
A stark, somber silence
For now was time to dine,
And a majestic banquet
Was arranged for them
With myriads of dishes,
With multitudes of cuisines
With many a beverages
With mouth-watering desserts
But the most savoury
Were the spongy burgers,

Stuffed with raw meat
Seasoned and garnished fittingly,
Upon which they unleashed their appetite
And started devouring them
But, after the first bite,
The taste irked them
And they demanded sauces,
For the burgers were not piquant.

But the sauce bottles
Were nowhere to be found
On the large banquet table
Although they ransacked
And plundered through it
And, then, all of them halted
And glared at her
And she felt mortified
For her sauce bottles
Were stolen the previous night
And instantly, she stood up
And scampered towards me
And whispered in my ears
In the most mellowed voice:
"Can I have some blood of yours?"
I let out a half-smile
And unbuttoned my chest,
Instantaneously she had
A slash at my bare bosom
With her whetted knife

And a pool of blood
Burst forth immediately
Which she contained
In an antique chalice
And went back to them
Rejoiced.

Thus, the banquet re-began
Along with the attendant noise
Soon, all the burgers,
Dipped and soaked and plated
With the hot blood-sauce,
Were ravenously devoured
Along with all the fares
Every bit and pieces of them
Yet none of them belched out
And started staring at her again
But she had nothing more to offer.

She hurtled back to me
And stole an inquiring glance
And I fell chagrined
I beckoned her to my side
And offered myself
As their remaining meal
If it pleased them at all
Thereupon, she kissed me
On my pale cheek
And said jubilantly —

"It will do sufficiently
For they are my close friends
They need to be treated well."

Now she went back to them
And came promptly back again
Escorted by a jubilant mob
Which offered me greetings
In a sub-human voice
Which I had never heard
Hitherto in my entire life
Yet I offered a bow
And glanced at her
She gestured with her eyes
As if to be saying, "Hurry up."
So I undressed myself,
Of that elegant suit
(Exclusively bespoke for this occasion)
From the neck to the feet
And stood stoically there
Akin to the nude artists
And, one by one, they came
With their forks and knives
With sharp and heavy choppers
And severed away the parts
They deemed most piquant
And chewed and munched
Or swallowed altogether
Not merely the flesh

But the bones, too,
Of my infirm breast
Of the forearm and fingers
Of the cheeks and neck
Of my thighs and shins
And all the sinews and muscles
Down to the liver and kidneys
And my still fluctuating lungs
And guzzled down all intestines
In uttermost exhilaration.

Thus the grand feast continued
Until only my assured eyes
(For they were riveted to her)
And my still living heart
(For she resided in there)
Were left in my skeleton
And here she yelled 'STOP'
In a high-pitched, shrill voice
And the guests got divided
Into two factions on either side
Making a clear passage
From me to my birthday girl
Through which she approached
With a smile so pure and innocent
That I forgot all my pains
And smiled back at her
But all at once
She delved deep into my eyes

With her penetrating gaze
And forked into my heart
Dead straight into the middle
And brought it out
With sheer surgical care
And placed it between her jaws
And pierced into it
With her glittering cuspids,
Still she emitted
Her sacred scarlet smile
But my eyes turned to stones
Forever.

23. The Marriage

He woke up delighted
Fresh from the morning dream
About a bright prospect,
A dream in which he saw
His soon would-be wife
Strolling with him
By the side of a placid lake
Amidst the sonorous symphony
Of the mermaids' singing
While the mermen showered
Their divine benediction
Upon the two in unison
While Neptune looked at them
And spelt his blessings.

The two soon to be united
Strolled for a length of time
Equivalent to Eternity
Or a little less than that
Or simply beyond Eternity
Amidst the blessed milieu
And spoke not a single syllable
Through their sealed lips

But reciprocated vows
Of their tender love
Only through their eyes
Which, though riveted elsewhere,
Saw only the image of the other
Without ever twinkling twice
Making each promise thrice
To seal it in fate's dice.

The dream was over
But he endeavoured to sleep
A little bit longer
To go back to the dream
Or simply draw to himself
Through the benign slumber
Or through the hangover
The remains of the dream
For he, though composed,
Felt a tinge of grief
Over the dream getting curtailed
Through his awakening,
For he wished the dream,
And the undisturbed stroll
With his would-be wife,
To go on forever and ever
Amidst the singing and the blessings
Of those mythical figures.

However, it was over
Though it was yet to be over,
Tonight the marriage would be
Earnestly solemnised,
So the slight tinge of sorrow
At the curtailment of the dream
Receded quickly into oblivion
And what remained
Was the prospect of the dream
Being translated into reality
By the late night tonight.

He got out of his bed
Yawning and gaping widely
Still subdued, although mildly,
With the languor of slumber
And straightaway began waiting
For the night to befall
And bring him closer altogether
To that moment of union
For which he had waited
For many a year long.

He went to the nearby pond
For the hymeneal bath
The rituals of which
Would take many an hour,
And as he reached the pond
He found its water

Strewn with flower petals
And the water itself
Appeared to have been tampered
With heavenly Elixir
Or the pond itself had
Got transubstantiated into
The brook of Lethe
Which would melt into oblivion
All the painful memories
Of his bygone days
After which lies for him
A series of paradisal bliss
The best of which would be
The long-coveted bridal kiss.

He unrobed himself
And dived into the water
And instantly found himself
Encircled by seven nymphs
But they were not singing
Neither did they utter
A single syllable or a word
But only encircled him
And kept looking at him
Who felt a succinct coyness
At their riveted gaze
And asked them in earnest
About why they were there,
And why at all did they appear?

Whom he had never seen before
Although he had bathed in the pond
Many a time foregone,
And went on to narrate to them
The dream in all its entirety
In which he had seen mermaids
Singing in a chorus
And also the benedictions
Showered upon by the mermen,
The blissful walking
By the side of his would-be wife,
The entirely heavenly ambience
Of the pastoral setting,
The panoramic vistas
Of the paradisal blessing.

The mermaids listened to him
All the while very attentively
And none of them dared
To intrude upon his speech
And then began to speak
In a succinct single voice:
"You are but a charming boy
Don't make yourself a playful toy
We have seen you many a time
Around this pond, amidst the vine
We have never intruded upon you
Though always felt drawn to you
You're like Phoebus burning bright

You shall set all wrongs to right
Today is but a blessed day
Do look charming and be gay
Tonight your marriage is solemnised
Tonight you'll be with your bride
Tonight will be a blissful night
And you will perform your nuptial rite
The countrymen all would be on their feet
And infants won't suck on mothers' teat
Yet there is something that is amiss
Would be revealed post your nuptial kiss
There is something you don't know yet
The catastrophe for which the stage is set
Dark clouds hovering over your fate
Beware of going to your mate
Don't go for your marriage tonight
Then, for you, things will be right."

Saying this, they all became air
Leaving no trace there
But he had questions to ask
About his nuptial prospect
And stood there in utter silence
Contemplating upon what they told
But heeded not their assertions bold
Although he felt the same tinge
That he had felt at
The curtailment of the dream
Yet he maintained his cheerful sheen

And divulged not a sign of sorrow
Or dejection or disappointment
And began ruminating upon
The bliss of his nuptial night
Of a future benign and bright.

Thus he came out of the pond
And dressed himself majestically
In the robes of the groom
For the time was now twilight
And he set out with emboldened gaits
For the countryside of his bride,
A long walk of many a mile
Escorted by the unseen presence
Of the music and symphony
Of a marriage procession
Which initially baffled him
For he could not trace
The source of that hymeneal band
But he fell overjoyed
With the invisible symphony
And kept on walking quietly
Under the overarching melody.

Night fell quick and sharp
It wasn't long before it was dark
A deep and stark blackness
Engulfed the entire ambience
Which startled him a bit

And he decelerated his pace
But then picked it up again
And walked briskly in the dark
But after many an hour walk
He needed to quench his thirst
And he looked all around
For a well or a pond
But he couldn't see one
Owing to the queer darkness
That has made his vision redundant
And he sat down dejected
On a large piece of stone
However, the music went on and on
Which now incensed him slightly
And he shouted "STOP" vehemently
But it could not be stopped
Only a voice out of the air
Spoke in a serene voice:
"The music is not to be ceased
Until your senses are fully freezed
We'll accompany you to the nuptial bed
We'll cease when you're fully fed."

He kept sitting there
In that dejected mood
Amidst those lively sounds
And the gruesome darkness
For a length of time
He himself could not gauge

And then there appeared
A swarm of fireflies
Who, out of compassion
Or invited by the music,
Came to his side,
Which offered him some solace
In that gloomy ambience,
And said in a chorus:
"We'll show you the way to the country
Which is the blessed land of peasantry
You'll be guided by our light
We shall fly and burn bright
We'll lead you to your destination
So be up and let go of procrastination
We do burn, and we do pray
We lead whoever is led astray
We are denizens of the night
We set all the wrongs to right
We were invited by the symphony
And found you here in utter agony
We can't give you water to drink
Yet can lend you ways to think
We are here for your aid
We'll fulfil what we've said."

So the fireflies led the way
Dancing and burning
And showing him the path
In that abysmal dark

And he rejoiced
At these majestic light-bearers
And now he could relish
The symphony and the music
Which had escorted him
From the time he set out
On this forlorn path
Towards the countryside
To meet his happy bride
To make her his true wife.

Many an hour thus went by
And at the conclusion of which
The swarm of fireflies
Ceased to move further
And switched their lights off
Making the milieu dark again
But the sounds still did remain
Now striking a sinister cord
With their high pitches
And their steep falls
Now mingled with
The sound of wolves' growling
Which startled him greatly
And he, too, stopped at once
And addressed the fireflies
"Why have you suddenly stopped?"
To which the fireflies quipped:
"This is the bound of our territory

Written in our books of history
To move further is to be dead
Pay heed to what is being said
From here begins the domain
Of the demi-god and sinister omen
Proceed from here with utter precaution
Heed your words and watch your action
The demi-god takes the lion's shape
And sucks out blood from the groom's nape
You are sure tonight's groom
Fate will sweep its musty broom
The countrymen are all on their feet
But no cuckoo sings, nor lambs bleat
They are waiting for your arrival
But are thinking of their own survival
The demi-god has disapproved the wedlock
They are terrified and are in shock
Still, you have not yet been denied
You don't look aghast or terrified
What's going on? We really don't know
Tonight the boar won't mate with the sow
Tonight is the night of many premonitions
All your stars are in whirly motions
Open your eyes and tread cautiously
Or you'll lose something very dearly
Don't hurry to be with your bride
Or you'll lose your nuptial pride
Let the marriage be earnestly solemnised
Let all its rites be fully ritualised

Let the dawn appear on the horizon
Then approach your bride with precision
For the demi-god lion lies in wait
For the groom to open the bride's gate
To consume all his nuptial bliss
And consummate his marriage with a kiss
Whatever happens after, we cannot tell
This would serve as a warning bell
We now say what the nymphs had said
A precaution in words aptly laid
You are but a charming boy
Don't make yourself a playful toy."

Saying this, the fireflies
Glided back to their safe abodes
Leaving him alone in the dark
Still, many a mile to tread
On these mazy meandering ways
But the only solace he could find
Was seeing a dim light afar
That twinkled in the dark
On the outskirts of the country
That was the village of the peasantry
Where lay the prospect of his destiny.

II

The sounds of the marriage procession
Have been reverberating
For many an hour
Each of them,
Being the length of Eternity
Bereft of any serenity
In the absolute absence
Of the pettiest magnanimity
Devoid of any profundity
But the ceaselessness of
It seamless continuity
Veneered all its monotony
And glossed over it
With a sheen of beauty.
But all it could concoct
Was an impression of vanity.

The countrymen had been
All on their feet
Since the arrival of the sound
Of the hymeneal band
The beating of the drums
The high-pitched clamour
Of trumpets and trombone
The milder, miserable notes
Of Shehnai and Sarangi
Yet they barely could gauze

The distance of those sounds
Merely stood looking
For the procession to arrive
Which, yet unseen, had sent
Its a signal of approaching
Through its sundry sounds
Which discreetly lent to ears
A note of delirious symphony
A stringent note of cacophony
Which imparted to the listeners
A profound sense of anxiety
A foreboding of an imminent doom,
However, bereft of any gloom
Put the hearts on tenterhook
Imparted to the youth
A decrepit, decimated look.

Terror-stricken to the core
And shaken to their marrows
They could take no more
And grew impatient
With their tense waiting,
For the syllables of time
Accompanied and escorted
By the piercing syllables
Of the musical instruments
Were just too much to endure
From which they, verily,
Intended to find a cure

In the endeavour to ensure
To cling on to the life
They had been living
Prior to the arrival
Of that marriage procession
Whose different errands
Had already taken months
And yet it was just
Too far from being over.

A young boy who partook
In the countrymen's vigil
Opined with succinctness
That they better seek
The foreseeing services
Of the old wise woman
Who had already warned
Of this marriage's doom
Who had opined to defer
The wedding rituals
And all its solemn rites
Until nine more moonless nights
In which the lion-shaped demi-god
Will have its nine kills
By the snowy hills
In the vicinity of the countryside
And will send a signal
Of its appeasement
Through the high-pitched roar

And then only the rituals
And all its sanctified ceremonies
Should be fairly instituted
And consummately concluded.

Thus they began to proceed
Towards her shabby hut
But every step of each one
Was accompanied with
Incantation of various gods
Whom they worshipped
And had deified
Through the sundry process
Of their social evolution
And had deposited
Their heart and soul
In their queer faith
About which they themselves
Knew next to nothing
Except for what now characterised
The involuntary yet calculated
Movement of their throbbing lips
Which uttered not a syllable
Known to Homo Sapiens.

Now the three-miles long march
Against the Night's Eternity
Came to a sudden halt
When the one leading the procession

With a bright lantern,
Whose wick was constantly quivering,
Made a gesture of silence,
Accompanied by a sibilant sound,
And beckoned to yonder hut
Which was enveloped in the entirety
In darkness ghastly
Of this long moonless night
Whose stillness was disturbed
By the indiscreet chatter
Of the countrymen in the procession
Or by the howling of wolves
Whose ever-intact pack
Lay in wait to pounce
On their luckless prey.

Now the young boy stepped ahead
And began marching in long gaits
Towards the wise woman's hut
Turning once and gesturing
To the country folks of the procession
To follow him in utter resignation
And not to make a single sound
And firmly stand their solid ground
And walk as if in ritualistic chore
And approach the wise woman's door.

The first knock went unanswered
Yet they did not panic once
For the dim rays of light
Coming from the window ajar
Reinforced their assurance
Vindicated their perseverance
In this nocturnal march
And lent a repose calm
To their throbbing hearts.
Then they knocked again
This second time, a little louder
Yet it met with the same fate
And none came to open the gate
Neither a soul moved inside
But only a wolf's howling
Was heard from a distance
And died in an instance
Yet it sent shivers down the spine
Of the ones in the procession
And panic began to set in
Within their heart's recess,
Still, they divulged no sign
Of their inward palpitation,
Endeavoured to conceal
This very queer trepidation,
Did barely succumb to speak
An unruly word of agitation
Still persevered to maintain
That posture of resignation.

Now came the third knock
After a long and heavy wait
And it did find an answer
From the inmate of the hut-
A sound of stern coughing
Pierced and penetrated
The night's ghastly stillness
And a sudden calmness
Transpired through the hearts
Of all the country folks
Who were hitherto unnerved
With the grim silence
That met their knockings
Who were at tenterhooks
About what the old woman
Was going to prophecies,
About what the marriage
Would befall the country folks,
About when the procession
Of marriage would arrive,
About when their lives
In normalcy would thrive,
About when this wretched night
Would come to be subdued,
About when this long
Lethargic wait would conclude,
About when the slithering
Of their fearful hearts
Would transubstantiate into

The rhythmic stirs
Of their satiated souls.
The door of the hut
Now opens with a creaking sound
Of all its hinges
And a decrepit woman
With a lantern in her hand
Suspended around her visage
Appears in a stoic posture
Without a word of greeting
And stands staring vacantly
Into the night's blackness
And said in a humble tone :
"I know what you intend to ask
But to answer is not my task
I know of all your inherent fear
When the lion would kill the deer
When the marriage procession arrives
When peace returns to the tribe
When its rites would conclude
When our hearts would joy-exude
When our lives to normalcy return
When our gestures won't be stern
When the demi-god would be appeased
When you would revel in your feast
When the bride goes to the groom
And would conclude the marriage's doom
When the night would have a moon
When we all would share the boon

When your hearts would find peace
And would drink life to the lees
When your soul would be satiated
And with delight is saturated."

An old man in the procession
Responded with utter precision,
"You've said what we could have
When the lion comes out of the cave
You are the wisest of us all
Save us from this imminent fall
You are now our only light
Our sole hope of a prospect bright
You've never been proven wrong
And have saved us from perdition long
Once again, we're at your door
Owing to some circumstances sore
We're in dire need of your aid
It has been true what you've said
The marriage would consume a prize
And would fill the country with cries
We've taken precautionary measures
Yet we can't fill all the fissures
It has been an unending wait
We are yet to predict our fate
We've been listening to its approach
The marriage procession is yet to encroach
Upon the bounds of the country
Through the ways various and sundry?"

Thus pleaded the old man
And curtailed his speech
With a sudden silence
And there ensued instantly
A deep and vigorous pause,
As if enjoining in the cause,
Thereupon the old woman,
Who had listened to his supplication
With a vacant expression,
Lowered her gaze upon the boy
And made a gesture to him
To come inside her hut
Along with the old man
And the rest to wait there outside
With which they instantly complied
Although they felt a little terrified.

Now the door was shut
With the same creaking sound
Of its loosened hinges
With which it had opened,
And there ensued another pause
After which the two emerged
From that dilapidated door
But the wise old woman
Didn't come to see them off
Yet they had a pronouncement
For the fellow country folks

From the decrepit woman
And thus began the old man:
"We have made a fatal mistake
We've taken what wasn't ours to take
We've complied to this marriage
To rest the serpent in our carriage
Now the doom is upon us all
We'll experience a grisly fall
Unless the demi-god is satiated
Our own hearts will remain agitated
The gruesome fate can be foiled
With seventy frogs in a cauldron boiled
The marriage mob is about to arrive
So, for our errands, we must strive
We have to be the best of hosts
And ward off all our inner ghosts
We must maintain a gleeful posture
And must not make a sorry gesture
We must take a lofty pride
Let the groom go to the bride
Let them enjoy their nuptial bliss
And seal their fate with a kiss
But let not their marriage be fully consummate
Otherwise, it would forfeit our fate
The groom must be taken away from the bed
And placed in a coffin made of lead
Carry the coffin to the lion's den
And wait for the cackling of the hen
If the cackling is heard by the dawn

Then we would have no reason to mourn
And if silence pervades the morn
Then the lamb is dreadfully shorn
However, in both the cases to be,
The curse would be lifted utterly
Whatever befalls our groom
It will save us from our doom
So, for our enterprise, we must strive
In the pit of hell, we all must dive."

III

Thus, he finally arrived
Escorted and accompanied
By the invisible hymeneal band
And the country folks rushed
To give him a welcoming grand
In their own pastoral land
But all they could see
Was a solitary bloke
In the groom's robe
Approaching them dejectedly
Looking into the dark vacantly
But the invisible source of sound
Surprised them greatly
As it did to the boy
Who, however, looked
Not so happy as a groom
But only walked along
With a drooping head
And a dolorous posture
Which lent him an uncanny texture.

The countrymen however
Put on a zealous demeanour
As the wise old woman had opined
And neither looked baffled
Nor did they appear terrified
At what they were seeing

Or what was yet to come,
Instead, they started dancing
To the tune of the invisible band
Encircling the solitary boy
Hugging and embracing him
One by one, many a time,
Subsuming into oblivion
All the premonitions and dread
They have been made aware of
By old woman's creed.

One of the countrymen
Enjoined the boy
To change his dress
And put on the attire of the groom
Which was a white robe
In accordance with
The customs of the country
Which perplexed him immensely
For he had already
Put on the groom's red robes
In accordance with
The custom of the city,
Still, he barely opposed
And gladly put them on
Along with the white shoes
And a crown on his head,
From which were suspended
Strings of various flowers

Down to his belly
Which all but concealed
His bright, boyish visage,
Which lent him the look
Of one perfect groom.

Now, one of the old man
Admonished him to walk
Alongside the village folks
Who marched towards
The village's sacred well
Whose holy water
Was supposed to purify
The body and the soul
And ward off and cure
All evil propensities
That penetrated one's core.

Finally, after a long march,
They reached the consecrated well
And bowed to it in earnest
Asking the boy to replicate
Their gesture of reverence
Which he did at last
And, thereafter, he was asked
To sit on a piece of stone
And they began to fetch
The well's water from its depths,
For its water had receded

Many a hundred feet down,
And poured it into a large cauldron
And put seventy frogs into it
And placed it on a hearth
Under which logs of timber
Were immediately set on fire,
And they all stepped aside
Waiting for the steam to rise.

The frogs in the cauldron
Were gay and dancing
And let out their croaking
In their high-pitched voice
But slowly and steadily
The croaking and the movements
Began to fade away
Leaving behind a trail
Of deep and sinister silence,
As the water reached
Its boiling point,
But what baffled the boy
Was that none of the frogs
Showed an ounce of resistance
Nor even endeavoured
To jump out of the cauldron
As the temperature rose,

But only surrendered meekly
As if they felt nothing
Until they were smoothly consumed
By the rising heat of the water.

Now the boy was adjured
To inhale the steam
Rising from the cauldron
And drink some of its water
Which he initially gainsaid
But eventually resigned himself
To their stern commands,
Which were imparted
Not through their voices
But through their gaze and glare
Which spoke through the silence,
Permeating and pervading the ambience
Which was abruptly broken
By the old man's utterance:
"You're now a groom to the bride,
To your bride, you now must strive
The marriage has been earnestly solemnized
You'll now be perpetually mesmerized
Your bride is primed for consummation
There is no cause for procrastination
You must hurry to your bride
And salvage your nuptial pride
Walk to her with a surer foot
Talk to her in a tender mood

Raise her veil with utter precision
Sing with her in utmost unison
Lend her frame a temperate touch
But don't you panic or fuss too much
Her virginity is now yours to take
Hurry to your bed, for glory's sake,
Hasten now to your grand new enterprise
Which would offer you a mighty surprise
Nothing lurks between you and your bride
So, to your bride, you now must strive."

Now they beckoned him
To a large mansion
That now stood solemnly
In their full-frontal view
Which baffled the boy exceedingly,
For he had hardly seen it
All the long while
He had been there,
Or it appeared to him
That it just conjured up there
Suddenly, out of the thick air,
And stood there majestically
With a sinister grandeur
That excited and frightened
Alike at the same instance,
For it had an uncanny structure
With its three large columns
(Instead of four columns

Suitable to geometrical pattern)
Shouldering its entire weight
From the three sides,
And at the top of each,
Shapes of the lion were
Marvellously sculpted
In the very act of killing
And devouring its prey at large,
But the most surprising aspect
Was that the bulging eyes
Of the sculpted lion
Glowed in the darkness
Like the eyes of a real lion
And imparted to the onlooker
A sense of gruesome terror.

Gradually, with uneasy steps
He approached the gate
Of this uncanny abode,
While the countrymen all
Waived their hands meekly
To send him off,
And he entered into it
Without any resistance whatsoever
And went straight through
A very narrow passageway,
That was scantily lit up,
That led to an underground chamber
Where he found a bed

With a girl sitting on it
In the apparel of a bride
But he could barely see
Anything very clearly
For the lack of ample light,
Though his heart beat faster
At the prospect of meeting
The one to be his wife,
His ladylove, his damsel bright.

As he stepped inside
This grand nuptial room
It lit up vigorously
From all sides and corners
With bright, effulgent lights
That, for a few moments,
Marred the boy's vision
And he could see nothing
And withdrew his eager steps
And stood his ground frozen,
And dared not move ahead
Until he regained his sight
Which took a fair bit of time,
And, as he opened his eyes
After that sudden blackout,
He found the dimensions
Of that large spacious room
To have been altered altogether
And all its sinister aspects

Had been entirely evaporated
And had been replaced
With the placid milieu
Of the legendary romances
Where the protagonist carves
His way through various ordeals
To attain that blessed union
With his fairy ladylove
Whose attainment remains
The sole purpose
Of his chivalrous campaigns.

Shaking off all his anxieties
And all his palpable fears
He approached his bride
With surer, swifter steps
With his rejuvenated soul
Thrilled at this grand endeavour
Of consummating his bride
For whom he had waited
For the length of Eternity
With a peculiar serenity
Although, at various times,
With an ounce of insanity
But always imbued with
A sense of celestial beauty
That imparted him levity

At the hours of extreme anxiety
Whose gruesome tenacity, at times,
Crippled him psychologically.

He sat down quietly
On the edge of the nuptial bed
Harbouring a turmoil
In the recess of his heart
And placed his hand
Ever so delicately
Upon that of hers
Whose visage was still veiled
With her wedding cloak
And who, upon his touch,
Shrunk and withdrew
Her hands involuntarily,
Out of coyness or modesty,
Although it appeared
She coloured moderately,
From under her veil
And changed her stance,
And moved away slightly
From her advancing bridegroom
Who, now with emboldened courtesy,
Approached and grabbed
Her soft ivory hands
And lifted her veil
From her silvery countenance
Which was embellished

With ornaments and jewels pristine
Of antique kinds and designs.

He now lay down on the bed
And pulled her to his side
And placed his lips upon hers
And sucked passionately
And then rubbed her temples
With his eager fingertips
And then slid downwards
Towards her neck and nape
And started licking at them
And smelled her bosoms
And placed his hands gently
Upon each after the other
Until he suddenly felt
Something piercing at his nape
With a vehement force
And, with quick reflexes,
He tried to jerk himself off
From the tenacious grip
That had got hold of him
With a superhuman force,
And after a long struggle
He freed himself from
Those disproportionately powerful clutches
And instantly pirouetted
To figure out his assailant
And to his bafflement

He found no one there
Except for his coveted bride
Who, by now, had taken off
Her bridal attires
And her bodily features
Had now appeared transfigured
Into that of a lion
Who let out a loud roar
And pounced upon the boy
Who, this time, did not
Endeavoured to escape
But only stood his ground
Gazing at the bride-beast
With a look truly sore
Until his innocent eyes
Could see no more.

With the first rays of dawn
The old man of the country
Enjoined all the country folks
To gather around him
And encircle him thrice
And pronounced the epilogue.

Epilogue

This is the hour of all our waiting
There is nothing in it for our taking
The rooster now calls from the east
We have satiated the murky beast
The marriage has been earnestly solemnised
The groom has been consumed by the bride.
The long, unending night is finally over
Still something threatens us from the bower
There is nothing in it for us to mourn
The lamb has already been brutally shorn
Still we are consumed with fears grave
We've lost our courage, we're not brave
The curse is yet to be lifted from us
This was ordained from the start as thus
The demi-god is now apparently appeased
Yet our fate is forfeited and seized
The lion had taken the bride's shape
And has sucked blood from the boy's nape
A new day now dawns on the horizon
But we'll keep suffering as much in unison
For our daily errands, we now must strive
On our daily death, we now must thrive
What relief at last it brings us then,
The lion will temporarily return to its den
Our prayers can fleetingly defer the bane
Hardly could we pronounce "Amen, Amen, Amen..."